The Nugents of Westmeath and Queen Elizabeth's Irish primer

Maynooth Studies in Local History

SERIES EDITOR Raymond Gillespie

This volume is one of five short books published in the Maynooth Studies in Local History series in 2016. Like their predecessors they range widely, both chronologically and geographically, over the local experience in the Irish past. Chronologically they span the worlds of 16th-century Westmeath to those of Waterford in the early 20th century. Geographically, they range across the length of the country from Derry and Antrim to Waterford and Mallow in County Cork. Socially they move from the landed and elite ecclesiastical society of Sir John Keane and Thomas Ward, dean of Connor, to the social position of children who lost their mother in 19th-century Mallow and trade unionism in Derry in the 20th century. In doing so they reveal diverse and complicated societies of the local past, and the range of possibilities open to anyone interested in studying that past. Those possibilities involve the dissection of the local experience in the complex and contested social worlds of which it is part as people strove to preserve and enhance their positions within their local societies. Such studies of local worlds over such long periods are vital for the future since they not only stretch the historical imagination but provide a longer perspective on the evolution of society in Ireland and help us to understand more fully the complex evolution of the Irish experience. These works do not simply chronicle events relating to an area within administrative or geographically determined boundaries, but open the possibility of understanding how and why particular regions had their own personality in the past. Such an exercise is clearly one of the most exciting challenges for the future and demonstrates the vitality of the study of local history in Ireland.

Like their predecessors these five short books are reconstructions of the socially diverse worlds of the poor as well as the rich, women as well as men, children as well as adults and reconstruct the way in which those who inhabited those worlds lived their daily lives, often little affected by the large themes that dominate the writing of national history. In addressing these issues, studies such as those presented in these short books, together with their predecessors, are at the forefront of Irish historical research and represent some of the most innovative and exciting work being undertaken in Irish history today. Like the other volumes in this series, they provide models that others can follow, and convey the vibrancy and excitement of the world of Irish local history today.

Maynooth Studies in Local History: Number 123

The Nugents of Westmeath and Queen Elizabeth's Irish primer

Denis Casey

FOUR COURTS PRESS

Set in 10pt on 12pt Bembo by
Carrigboy Typesetting Services for
FOUR COURTS PRESS LTD
7 Malpas Street, Dublin 8, Ireland
www.fourcourtspress.ie
and in North America for
FOUR COURTS PRESS
c/o ISBS, 920 N.E. 58th Avenue, Suite 300, Portland, OR 97213

ISBN 978–1–84682–608–5

Printed in Ireland
by eprint, Dublin.

Contents

Acknowledgments

There is so much that can be said about Christopher Nugent's primer for Queen Elizabeth I that this short book can only hope to scratch the surface of a limited number of issues relating to it. However, I thought I should write *something* about it now, rather than postponing it in favour of writing (or rather not writing) a larger book down the line. As Ernest Hemingway wrote in *Death in the afternoon*, 'if I had waited long enough I probably never would have written anything at all since there is a tendency when you really begin to learn something about a thing not to want to write about it but rather to keep on learning about it always'.

This book began as a paper delivered to the annual colloquium of the Henry Sweet Society for the History of Linguistic Ideas in 2011 and I would like to thank the organizer, Dr Deborah Hayden (Maynooth University), for the opportunity to speak at it. Likewise, I have presented aspects of this research to various audiences in recent years, and I would like to extend my gratitude to the convenors and organizers of the Cambridge Group for Irish Studies (Magdalene College, Cambridge), the Anglo-Saxon, Norse and Celtic Research Seminar (Cambridge), the Centre for Medieval and Renaissance Studies (Trinity College, Dublin) and the Biennial Conference of the Society for Renaissance Studies (University of Manchester).

A good deal of the research upon which this book is based was completed during 2011–12, when I had the good fortune of receiving a postdoctoral fellowship from the Society for Renaissance Studies, which I held at the Department of Anglo-Saxon, Norse and Celtic in the University of Cambridge. Without their support not only would this book never have been written, but it is doubtful that I would have continued in academia; heartfelt thanks must go to Dr Sarah Alyn Stacey (Trinity College, Dublin), Dr Alexander Samson (University College, London), and, in particular, Professor Máire Ní Mhaonaigh (Cambridge). It was completed at the Department of Early Irish, Maynooth University, to whose members I am also grateful, particularly Dr Elizabeth Boyle and Professor David Stifter.

Various libraries and librarians have also been very generous with their collections and time over the years, and in particular I would like to acknowledge the help of the staff of the Benjamin Iveagh Guinness Library at Farmleigh House (where the primer is kept), the libraries of the Royal Irish Academy, Trinity College, Dublin, and the National Library of Ireland. I am grateful for permission to reproduce a photograph of the primer on the cover; the image of

f. 4v of Benjamin Iveagh Library IV D1, copyright Marsh's Library, Dublin, was supplied by the Irish Script On-Screen project of the School of Celtic Studies, Dublin Institute for Advanced Studies. In Cambridge thanks must be extended to the Parker Library (Corpus Christi College), St John's College library, the Faculty of English library and the Manuscripts and Rare Books reading rooms of the Cambridge University Library. In addition, I would like to thank the series editor, Professor Raymond Gillespie, for accepting this book for inclusion in the Maynooth Studies in Local History series, and Professor Damian McManus (Trinity College, Dublin) and Dr Marc Caball (University College Dublin) for their various comments on aspects of this work over the years.

Lastly, I would like to thank the Casey and Conroy families for their support over so many years. Needless to say, none of the above are responsible for the mistakes, omissions, lapses and sheer ignorance that pepper these pages.

Introduction

When Elizabeth II spoke five words of Irish at a state banquet held in her honour in Dublin Castle in 2011 (two of which were the same (the vocative particle, *a*)) she was treated to rapturous applause by the assembled guests.[1] It was a gesture that her namesake and predecessor, Elizabeth I, knowing that language and language use are emotive issues, would have appreciated; it was also as much spoken Irish as either Elizabeth are ever likely to have attained.

During her visit, Elizabeth II was given a gift of a facsimile of a 16th-century primer or guide to the Irish language. That undated primer – the subject of this book – represents the first sustained attempt to offer instruction in aspects of the Irish language to a non-Irish speaker, and is a landmark (albeit a neglected one) in the history of cultural exchange in 16th-century Ireland.[2] Although the primer is a document of great cultural and political significance – and one which is frequently noted in passing – it has hitherto escaped detailed analysis.[3] It was commissioned for Elizabeth I by a young Anglo-Irish noble named Christopher Nugent (a future baron of Delvin, Co. Westmeath), probably around 1564, while he was a student at the University of Cambridge. However, she almost certainly never read it, which is implied by the manuscript's lack of contemporary marginalia and its discovery at Madingly Hall (near Cambridge) in the middle of the 19th century. It was subsequently sold a number of times, before finally being acquired by Benjamin Guinness (3rd earl of Iveagh), and is now housed in the library of Farmleigh House, Dublin.

The primer is much more than a rough guide to learning Irish; it is a lens through which a variety of contemporary and historical traditions and concerns may be investigated.[4] It speaks to the interests of its commissioner (Nugent) and intended audience (Elizabeth) – neither of whom were directly interested in promoting the Irish language – and to their wider worlds. It is the confluence of this multiplicity of interests and influences that make the primer a fascinating object of study.

This study has three principal aims, which are reflected in its organization. First, it will offer a local historical perspective for the document, anchoring the primer's production within the history of its author's family (first chapter) and the story of his own life (second chapter). Secondly, it will explore the primer's linguistic contexts, looking at how it fitted into changing attitudes to the Irish language during the 16th century (third chapter) and exploring it as a product of the medieval Irish grammatical tradition and of Renaissance second-language teaching (fourth chapter). Finally, the first ever section-by-section analysis of the contents of the primer will be undertaken (fifth chapter).

The first two chapters will explore the background and career of Christopher Nugent, baron of Delvin, the primer's commissioner and possible author. The Nugents were among the most important Anglo-Irish families, with their lands centred upon Delvin (now Co. Westmeath), on the edge of the Pale. Proud of their English heritage and their descent from some of the earliest colonists, they had close familial, political and economic links with many of the premier aristocratic families of Ireland. Their engagement with Gaelic culture is demonstrated by their sponsorship of Irish poets and by the poetic accomplishment, in both Irish and English, of Christopher's brother, William. Christopher Nugent was 14 when his father (the baron of Delvin) died in 1559 and he became a ward of the governor/lord deputy of Ireland, Thomas Radcliffe (3rd earl of Sussex). He was sent to the University of Cambridge where he matriculated as a fellow-commoner of Clare Hall (now Clare College) in 1563, and was most likely presented to Queen Elizabeth I when she visited the university in 1564, shortly after which he apparently produced his undated primer. He returned to Ireland soon afterwards, and although generally loyal to the government, he was frequently the object of suspicion owing to his recusancy and the activities of various associates and family members, and he eventually died in prison in 1602.

In the third chapter, issues relating to languages in Ireland and England will be examined, with particular attention given to the place of the Irish language in practical politics and religious discourse during the 16th century. Although Elizabeth I may have supported moves towards proselytizing in Irish and the production of Protestant printed material in Irish, the cause was not universally .espoused, nor was Irish ever intended to be granted parity with English or Latin. In the primer's introduction, Christopher Nugent shows his awareness of these contemporary discourses through his references to the political benefits of a linguistically 'liberal' policy. He assiduously stayed clear of religious considerations; Christopher Nugent was Catholic during a tumultuous period and as divisions sharpened the Nugents were fated to become some of the most notable Old English recusants.

The two main influences upon the primer – the Irish bardic grammatical tradition and Renaissance linguistic scholarship – are the subjects of the fourth chapter. Although there is no conclusive proof that the Irish-speaking Christopher Nugent received his early education in a bardic environment, it is quite possible he received some instruction in that tradition, especially as the famous poet Giolla Brighde Ó hEódhasa (*ob.* 1614) claimed to have been educated alongside Christopher's brother, William. In addition to drawing upon an Irish bardic grammatical tradition that had existed since at least the 8th century, the primer is very much a Renaissance document in layout and design, and its Cambridge context has been greatly under-appreciated (as will be seen when comparing it to the primer *Aibidil Gaoidheilge & Caiticiosma* of Nugent's Cambridge contemporary, Seaán Ó Cearnaigh).

In the final chapter, the contents of the primer will be subject to a close examination. The primer is an extremely short document, consisting of only 12 folios, of which only nine contain text. It comprises of a Dedication (ff 2r–4v, in English), an 'Originall of the nation' (a history of the Irish people and language, in Latin) (ff 5r–7v), an alphabet (f. 8r), division of vowels and consonants (f. 8v), list of 'diphthongs' (f. 9r), word list of 12 items in Irish, Latin and English (ff 9v–10r) and a phrase list of six items, in the same three languages (f. 10v). It does not contain many of the features a modern teacher or learner might consider necessary in a second language instruction tool, such as paradigms of verbs and nouns; it was – to use a phrase applied to the approach of the 17th-century Czech educator Jan Amos Comenius – 'loose bricks without mortar'.[5]

1. The Nugents of Delvin in medieval and early modern Ireland

Christopher Nugent's ancestor and founder of the Nugent line, Gilbert de Nugent (1st baron of Delvin), was of the line of the lords of Nogent de Rotrou (Nogent-le-Rotrou) in Normandy,[1] and settled in Ireland's midlands thanks to the generosity of the great Norman magnate Hugh de Lacy (*ob.* 1184).[2] Gilbert married de Lacy's sister (Rose) and received Delvin for the service of five knights.[3] The pattern of subinfeudation of de Lacy's holdings was in keeping with the practice of utilizing existing political units, with de Lacy's charter granting Gilbert the lands 'which the O'Finelans held in the time of the Irish' (i.e., the territory of the Ó Finnalláin kingdom of Dealbhna Mhór, modern Co. Westmeath).[4] Hugh is also said to have given unspecified lands to Gilbert's brother, Richard de Capella.[5] The 17th-century genealogist An Dubhaltach Mac Fhirbhisigh recorded alternate claims that Gilbert was either a brother-in-law or a nephew of de Lacy and that he obtained the barony of Delvin as a dowry or through force.[6] Gilbert left no legitimate heir (but an illegitimate son of his sired a number of minor Nugent lines) and he was succeeded by his brother, Richard, who in turn left a daughter, Catherine, as heiress.[7] She married Richard de Tuite, who took the name Nugent, and whose line continued until the late 14th century.[8] By the 1380s the direct line had again died out and another heiress named Katherine married into a collateral branch of the Nugent family, with her husband (William, son of Nicholas) assuming the title baron of Delvin, by right of his wife.[9] William was subsequently prominent in local judicial and military matters in the 1390s and 1400s, serving as a justice of the peace and sheriff of Co. Meath (Co. Westmeath not then existing).[10] The Nugents continued to be active in royal service in the 15th century and Richard Nugent (10th baron of Delvin, *ob.* 1475) rose to serve as deputy-lieutenant of Ireland (1444–5 and 1448–9).[11] He was succeeded as baron by his son, Christopher, whose commercial interests included establishing a guild of glovers and skinners in Dublin city in 1476.[12] His son, Richard fitz Christopher Nugent (*ob.* 1538), was 12th baron and served as deputy to the lord deputy, in 1527–8 and again in 1534, like his grandfather before him. However, his period of office was not an unqualified success, as evinced by a 1528 letter from the archbishop of Dublin and the chief justice to Henry VIII's chief minister, Cardinal Wolsey, in which they protested that Nugent was an oppressor rather than a protector of the people.[13] They complained that the relative smallness of Nugent's landed resources required him to lean more on the Palesmen than the much richer earl of Kildare (the regular lord deputy) would have done in the normal course of events. Things went from bad to worse when Richard was captured by Kildare's Gaelic Irish ally O'Connor Faly in May 1528, and not released until the following year.[14] Despite these setbacks, he was again briefly appointed acting deputy upon the resignation (and rebellion) of the earl's son, Lord Offaly ('Silken Thomas'), in 1534.

Among the enormous political and social consequences of the fall of the house of Kildare in the 1530s (following Silken Thomas' rebellion), was the refusal of the crown henceforth to grant the lord deputyship to any Anglo-Irish noble, closing off that avenue of opportunity for families like the Nugents. However, they did not fall from favour, nor was their regional importance diminished – if anything it may have grown in stature, thanks to the development of a power vacuum that lasted until the full restoration and return of the 11th earl of Kildare under Queen Mary (1556), which left the government increasingly reliant upon the Nugents to police the borders of the Pale against Gaelic Irish attacks.[15] In 1552 Christopher's father was praised in a letter by the lord deputy and lord chancellor to the privy council for being 'very active in the service of the king',[16] and again in 1558, Lord Deputy Sussex wrote to Queen Mary asking her to confirm a grant made by Edward VI (1547–53) to Christopher's father, on account of the nobility and venerability of his lineage, his ancestors' contribution to the governing of the lordship, and because 'his wytte and habylyte to serve is ryght good'.[17]

Like almost any noble family, the Nugents also exercised ecclesiastical patronage. In the early 16th century they played an important role in the ecclesiastical life of the midlands, patronising and filling the upper echelons of the ecclesiastical establishments of Fore, Multyfarnham and Tristernagh, and extending their influence well into the diocese of Kilmore (in the Gaelic Irish O'Rourke and O'Reilly lordships of Bréifne).[18] The Henrician dissolution of the monasteries proved something of a windfall, as considerable tracts of surrendered monastic lands wound up in their hands. In some cases they continued to support the supressed orders.[19] An excellent example of the power they could wield as lay protectors on the ground may be seen in the patronage of Multyfarnham by Christopher Nugent (the primer's author) and his son Richard (1583–1642).[20] Elizabeth I complained that Multyfarnham was a centre of conspiracy during the Nine Years War,[21] and Sir Francis Shane protested that it was 'the nursery of all mischievous practices',[22] but later the Franciscan Hugh Ward lauded it as 'an ark in the deluge'.[23] All acknowledged that its protection stemmed from government reluctance to offend the Catholic barons of Delvin, for by-and-large the Nugents remained Catholic and only one important family member conformed; Nicholas Nugent (Christopher's uncle) became a staunch Protestant but it was not enough to save him when he faced trumped-up treason charges, and he was executed in 1582.[24]

THE NUGENTS' ENGLISH IDENTITY

In later medieval Ireland (after the 12th-century invasion) one of the most important marks of identity was paternal ancestry. Irish-language sources used the labels *Gaedhil* and *Gaill*, to denote a person's/group's patrilineal descent from either Míl of Spain (the fictitious pre-Christian invader of Ireland), or from the more recent invaders, respectively. Patrilineal descent was but one component of identity and should not be confused or made synonymous with political allegiance, linguistic preference/upbringing or dress (to name but a few other identity markers). In short, there were multiple forms of identity in medieval Ireland; to imagine an island populated by independent-minded Gaelic lords and diametrically opposed loyal English lieges (precisely divided by ancestry, political allegiance, culture and language) is as reductive as imagining those English settlers outside the Pale to have become 'more Irish than the Irish themselves', in contrast to a 'purer' east-coast brethren enveloped in an English cocoon. The complexities of identity can be imagined in the form of a Venn diagram, in which a multiplicity of factors overlapped, whose circles were not static, but subject to growth, shrinkage and realignment. Identities may have varied from location to location and generation to generation, and features could be actively promoted or suppressed, through performance or concealment, depending on the audience and desired outcome (as will be seen in the example of Shane O'Neill, later). This is evident in Christopher Nugent's primer, in which he stresses his English identity indirectly through referring to the Gaelic Irish as 'other', using phrases like 'from whence *they* came, & *theire* tongue deryued', and to the 'englyshe natione borne &bredd in England', with the implication that he is one of the English nation born and bred outside of England.[25] Nonetheless he simultaneously traded on Gaelic aspects of his own identity that made him qualified to offer Elizabeth a means of learning the Irish language.

In the contested terminology of medieval/early modern historiography the Nugents might be termed 'Anglo-Irish', a term initially intended to label those descended from the early invaders/settlers in the male line who maintained their English characteristics, but which has popularly come to be employed as a means of highlighting their supposed differences from both their Gaelic neighbours and their brethren in England, while simultaneously implying that they internalized aspects of both these groups.[26] Issues concerning the gradual Gaelicization of the invaders/settlers have long been topics of debate,[27] but as Kenneth Nicholls has argued, 'To speak of the "Gaelicization of the Normans" as if it were an external process, without taking into account the fact that many – perhaps most – of the people in question belonged by birth as much to one race as to the other, is to place the process of assimilation in a false perspective'.[28] All Gaelic Irish and Anglo-Irish lords were the product of matrimonial alliances between native and newcomer to one degree or another, and many were quite willing to use aspects of English or Irish culture and law when it suited their purposes. For example, in the middle of the 14th century, the Anglo-Irish 3rd earl of Desmond (Gerald fitz Maurice, also known as Gearóid Iarla) wrote Irish-language poetry,[29] while his contemporary Gaelic Irish neighbour, Cormac Mac Carthaigh (*ob.* 1359), received an extensive grant of lands from the justiciar, Sir Thomas Rokeby, in 1356.[30] Furthermore, Gaelic Irish lords, as Nicholls has argued, did not consider English sovereignty disagreeable provided it remained nominal, and in this they were not too far removed in practice from some (if not many) of their Anglo-Irish neighbours.[31] However, despite this frequent pragmatism, Steven Ellis is quite right to stress that the English identity professed by the 'English by blood' (to use the somewhat pejorative late medieval term) in Ireland cannot be gainsaid.[32]

By the 16th century the Anglo-Irish Nugents were occasionally being referred to by the government as a 'sept', a term normally reserved by the administration for Gaelic Irish families.[33] To some degree the consequences of financial decisions may have influenced external views on the Nugents' outward Gaelicization; they, like other Pale lords, had settled Gaelic Irish tenants as smallholders on their lands, as it was easier to squeeze them for rents and exactions than their Anglo-Irish tenants.[34] If the government could apply descriptors used for the Gaelic Irish to the Nugents, then Mac Fhirbhisigh went one step further, recording a fanciful tradition that the Nugents were descended from Conchobar, son of the high-king of Ireland, Tairdelbach Ua Conchobair (*ob.* 1156), thus actually making them *Gaedhil*, not *Gaill*.[35] This was not an isolated approach to the ancestry of a prominent old settler family, but an example of a type of family tree grafting that a number of (predominantly Catholic) Anglo-Irish families experienced in the early modern period, whereby they were furnished with spurious Gaelic origins.[36]

The extent to which the Nugents may be said to have been 'Gaelicized' (itself a nebulous concept) must be approached with caution. As already noted, their colonial roots ran deep, they held various important government offices, and had reasonably substantial landed and commercial interests within the colony, while they were also among the families whose names feature most prominently in the legal profession before 1600.[37] In the ecclesiastical sphere, the careers of members like Bishop Edmund Nugent of Kilmore were advanced by the government in the 1520s, specifically because they were seen as reliable and enthusiastic agents of Anglicization who were nonetheless acceptable to the Gaelic Irish.[38] A key reason for Edmund's success was that he was almost certainly a competent Irish speaker, a characteristic that is often taken as one of the most significant markers of Gaelicization.

THE NUGENTS AND THE IRISH LANGUAGE

Although ancestry was the litmus test for 'Englishness', language and language use were important (and emotive) issues in colonial (and extra-colonial) identity.[39] Famously exemplified in the Statutes of Kilkenny (1366), the surviving acts of medieval Irish parliaments contain repeated condemnations of the use of the Irish language and the concomitant 'degeneracy' that its use engendered in the colonists.[40] Such legislation also extended to the prohibition of other features of Gaelic culture among the Anglo-Irish community, such as Gaelic dress and sports. Repeated condemnations of the Irish language in particular merely testifies to the ubiquity of its presence and the very men who sat in parliament and enacted this punitive linguistic legislation between the 13th and 16th centuries were often Irish speakers themselves (such as the aforementioned earl of Desmond). Ambiguous linguistic attitudes mirrored wider societal blurring and by the 16th century the Irish language and Gaelic culture were established parts of the heritage of many among the Anglo-Irish communities.[41] Nonetheless not all partook of this common culture (or even its linguistic components) to the same degree; for example, the Nugents of Delvin may have patronized Gaelic poets on occasion, but there are no surviving poems to indicate that the Fitzgerald earls of Kildare did so. This is not to say that the Fitzgeralds held themselves aloof from Gaelic Ireland; on the contrary they were as intimately connected with the great Gaelic families as the Nugents were, if not more so. Christopher Nugent's claim (at the beginning of the primer) that the English-born Elizabeth Zouche felt the need to learn Irish when she married the future earl of Kildare (in 1503) is an indicator that a sound grasp of the Irish language was at the very least advantageous in Kildare's household at the beginning of the 16th century.[42]

However, the Nugents use of the Irish language must not be considered evidence of a preference for Gaelic over English cultural norms, nor of their jettisoning of their English identity in favour of a Gaelic one. The location of the barony of Delvin on the edge of the Pale (the latter being one of the few areas in Ireland where the king's writ continued to run regularly) meant their interconnectivity in the colonial and Gaelic worlds is unsurprising. Familial links with prominent Gaelic and Anglo-Irish families (through marriage and fosterage) and economic arrangements undoubtedly made it expedient for the Nugents to speak Irish, yet it need not have been their default language.[43] During Richard Nugent's captivity in 1528–9 O'Connor Faly permitted the earl of Ormond's son to visit his prisoner, but insisted that the interlocutors spoke Irish, which indicates that while he took it for granted that they would be fluent in Irish, he may have expected them to converse in English by default.[44] The strongest evidence for the Nugents' engagement with the Irish language and Gaelic culture is found in the examples of bardic poetry of which they were the patrons, subjects or authors. In this pinnacle of Gaelic literary art, we find Christopher's father – in good standing with the establishment during his lifetime – the subject of an Irish poetic elegy after his death in 1559.[45] The most prominent artefact testifying to the Nugent's engagement with Gaelic culture is the dubiously titled *Duanaire na Nuinseannach* ('The Nugent Poem-Book') – at least one section of which is dated from a loyalist perspective, *Anno domini 1577 7 an ixmadh bliadhain .x. do quuiin Isibél a rígheacht hShaxan 7 Éireann* ('the year of the Lord 1577 and the nineteenth year of Queen Elizabeth's being ruler of England and Ireland')[46] – and which was probably once owned by William Nugent (Christopher's brother).[47] Among its contents is a poem by Muircheartach Ó Cobhthaigh in which Christopher, like his father before him, is praised in traditional style for his liberality toward the poets and battle prowess (with commensurate generosity, Muircheartach suggested that Christopher should be awarded an earldom).[48] The poetic accomplishment of the *duanaire*'s owner (William Nugent) in Irish (as well as English) is well documented.[49] Nonetheless, his employment of a Gaelic cultural medium should not be taken simply as proof of 'Gaelicization'. William's poetry did not merely ape bardic style and sensibilities, it helped break new ground in the conception and expression of a territorially based collective Irish identity and has been characterized as displaying 'an Anglo-Norman mind-set which encompassed inclusive ethnicity in the context of a consciousness of territorial integrity'.[50] His English-language poetry (although it does not survive) appears to have been popular and was commended by critics like Richard Stanihurst.[51] English-language verse was as much a part of the Nugents' oeuvre as Irish, and William's son, Richard, was noted for composing the first English-language sonnet sequence written by an Irishman, *Cynthia*.[52] Many (if not all) of the Nugents were conversant with Gaelic culture and spoke the Irish language, yet the weight of evidence points to an Anglo-Irish family that was comfortable in a variety of cultural environments, but who would never have been inclined to place emphasis upon the second element of that contested hyphenated term, Anglo-Irish.

2. Delvin, Cambridge and Dublin Castle's dungeon: Christopher Nugent, baron of Delvin (1544–1602)

It was into the culturally diverse world outlined in chapter one that Christopher Nugent, eldest son of Richard Nugent (baron of Delvin, *ob.* 1559) and his wife Elizabeth Preston (daughter of Jenico Preston, Viscount Gormanston), was born in 1544. Not much can be said for certain of his early life, although it seems probable that he was educated first in his parents' household, and a claim by the poet Giolla Brighde (Bonaventura) Ó hEódhasa that he (Giolla Brighde) was educated alongside Christopher's brother, Richard, suggests that Christopher too probably received instruction in written Irish in a bardic environment or from a practicing poet.[1] It may be inferred that his knowledge of Latin was also acquired during that period, as the Latin section of his primer is probably too accomplished for a beginner learning it at university. The Elizabethan statutes of the University of Cambridge (1570) forbade the teaching of Latin grammar, insisting that adequate grammatical knowledge should be a prerequisite for matriculation, so Nugent was most likely competent in the language before matriculating there in his late teens.[2] It is not known what his Latin education consisted of, although the possible school books listed in the library of the 8th and 9th earls of Kildare hint at what was available in an aristocratic household a generation earlier.[3] Since that time there was probably an increase in the availability of printed instruction books in Ireland; as early as 1545 a James Dartas of Dublin is recorded as bulk buying books from London, including primers.[4] He appears to have been a regular and valued customer of his supplier, purchasing 73 primers, in English and Latin, of varying grades.[5] It is also conceivable (though unprovable) that Nugent was educated in a formal school, such as the cathedral school of St Patrick's in Dublin, where schoolmasters teaching grammar are recorded regularly from the middle of the 1550s.[6] His written English does not exhibit features of any of the antiquated dialects of English spoken in parts of the colony, some of which survived into the 18th century;[7] it is that of an educated Tudor noble or gentleman.

Christopher was 14 when his father died in 1559,[8] and he became a ward of the chief governor/lord deputy, Thomas Radcliffe (3rd earl of Sussex), in March 1563.[9] This may not have been unusual for a member of the family as

the Nugents held their lands directly from the crown.[10] Within two months
Christopher's guardian had packed him off to Cambridge, where he matriculated
as a fellow-commoner of Clare Hall on 12 May 1563;[11] sending the young
Nugent to Cambridge may have been part of Sussex's general policy of trying
to de-Gaelicize the Anglo-Irish.[12] The undated primer was probably composed
the following year, shortly after Elizabeth I's visit to the university, as implied
in the introduction in which he claimed 'it pleasyde your maiestie (whiche I take
aspetiall fauor) to comaunde me delyuer your Highnes the Iryshe Caracters with
instructions for reading of the language'.[13]

It has been suggested that Elizabeth's request may have been prompted by
an incident two years previously, when Shane O'Neill, the greatest of the
Gaelic Irish chiefs, visited Whitehall to render his submission.[14] Elizabeth was
noted for being able to greet dignitaries in their own languages but was not
able to do so in Irish, and consequently O'Neill provided written versions of
his submission in Irish and English, reasoning that 'my speeche beinge Irishe is
nott well understood'.[15] It has been speculated that Elizabeth may subsequently
have considered it politically expedient to obtain a rudimentary grasp of Irish.[16]
There is no way of proving this hypothesis, nor is there any indication (beyond
the above-quoted remark from the primer) that Elizabeth sought out Nugent
to provide her with instruction in Irish. A more likely scenario is that Elizabeth
made an off-the-cuff comment to the effect that she was interested in Irish and
Nugent saw an opportunity to ingratiate himself with the queen, and seized
it. Such an occasion would most likely have occurred when Elizabeth visited
Cambridge in 1564.

CHRISTOPHER NUGENT AT CAMBRIDGE

Christopher Nugent matriculated at the University of Cambridge at a time
when the growing perception of the importance of universities to the secular
and religious life of the state fostered a utilitarian attitude towards education.[17]
The good offices of powerful and influential alumni had saved the university
from abolition during Henry VIII's reign, after which it increasingly became
a factory for the 'apparatchiks of the Tudor State'.[18] Indeed, the university
experienced considerable growth while Nugent attended it during the first half
of the 1560s,[19] and he was among a steadily increasing cohort of Cantabrigians
who were acutely conscious of their future potential to shape national (and
possibly international) events. The decision to enrol him in Clare Hall was
probably that of his guardian, the earl of Sussex, a man both linguistically
competent and religiously indifferent.[20] During his tenure in Ireland, Sussex
was practical enough to realize the benefits of having Irish speakers in his
service; for example, his chaplain was later described by Hugh Brady, bishop of
Meath, as a learned preacher in Irish[21] (as was Brady himself),[22] although there

is no indication that Sussex learned even the rudiments of the language himself. Unlike contemporary concerned parents, who selected colleges and tutors in expectation of appropriate teaching and religious indoctrination, Sussex may have viewed Clare Hall as an appropriate place to keep his young ward out of serious trouble for a few years.[23] Indeed, the university's regulations were geared towards reining in the activities of potentially truculent aristocratic students, rather than their poorer brethren.[24] The expectations of (and those imposed on) aristocratic students – who did not necessarily need to study for a degree or profession – were quite different from those of poorer students, who saw the university as a gateway to a career in the church or the law.[25] However, although there was no set idea about what an aristocratic student should study, the university was far from being a holiday camp for the rich and idle. Students like Nugent would expect to inherit considerable landed and commercial interests eventually; a high standard of literacy (in at least English and Latin) and some rhetorical ability would be necessary to manage estates and pursue the litigation that frequently clogged Tudor courts and correspondence alike. Such skills were also necessary should they wish to enter royal service.[26]

The extent to which Christopher Nugent (and his primer) was influenced by developing educational trends and religious controversies at this time is unclear. Nugent can hardly have been unaware of religious tensions within the university and outside it, and it is possible (though unprovable) that his tenure in Cambridge served to strengthen his Catholicism. However, it is easy to overstate the immediate impact of contemporary religious disputes, and Cambridge need not have been an uncomfortable place for a Catholic like Nugent in the early 1560s.[27] Elizabeth's own faith was an eclectic mix of Lutheran ideas packaged in a traditional Catholic format, and English or Irish Catholics were not being forced until the papal bull of 1570 to choose between their loyalty to the crown or to Rome.[28] Elizabeth had been on the throne for slightly less than five years and to contemporaries it must have been uncertain whether the Elizabethan religious settlement of the 1560s would be any more permanent than those of Henry, Edward or Mary. The situation was epitomized by the cautiously conservative visitation (a kind of formal audit) of the university in 1559 by the new chancellor, Elizabeth's close advisor William Cecil (later Lord Burghley),[29] and it was not until the 1570s that the crown seems to have actively involved itself in Cambridge life.[30]

Given the paucity of information regarding Nugent's time spent at Cambridge, it is difficult to assess the effect university life had upon him. Nonetheless, evidence for a positive university experience is implied in a memorandum on abuses and suggested remedies in Ireland, apparently written while under confinement in England (see below), almost twenty years after Elizabeth's visit to Cambridge (26 May 1584).[31] Among the 'Certayne causes, generall, efficient, and privative, which helpe to wurke the distruction of Irelande', he noted:

The want of an Universitie to trayne up the yowth, in myne opynion, one of the cheifest causes of mischeif in the realme. For as ignorance leavethe a mann to his naturall appetite, wherin he little differethe from that of brute beasts, so knowledge leadeth him to vertue, by meane wherof he is made to know God, observe lawes, and desire to lyve orderlie, the things which specially do upholde all common weales throwgh the worlde that floorishe; the want wherof breedeth disobedience, disobedience contencion, contencion devision, devision destruction, according the sainge of Our Lord: Omne regnum in se divisum desolabitur et domus supra domum cadet.[32]

CHRISTOPHER NUGENT AND ELIZABETH AT CAMBRIDGE (1564)

If Nugent did produce the primer at Elizabeth's request, it is most likely that he did so when (or shortly after) Elizabeth visited the university during her summer progress of 1564.[33] These summer progresses were propagandistic exercises in image making, intended to establish and maintain her popularity and they occurred almost every year until the end of the 1570s.[34] In reality they were confined to the least-disaffected parts of the country (for example, she never ventured into the north) and were, as Jean Wilson has noted, 'propaganda for the faithful, not gestures of goodwill to the potentially hostile'.[35] At the time of Elizabeth's visitation in 1564 (5–10 August), the university was out of term but it was obliged to act out the day-to-day routine of term life for the queen.[36] It has been estimated that there were 1,267 residents in the university[37] and the various dignitaries that followed Elizabeth (and sections of her household) were lodged around the town, while she stayed at King's College.[38] Among them, her first cousin, Lord Hunsdon (George Carey, grandson of Thomas Boleyn), stayed at Nugent's college (Clare Hall), while Nugent's legal guardian, the earl of Sussex, stayed at St Catherine's College, which would suggest that Nugent's enrolment at Clare Hall was not due to particularly close links between it and the earl.[39] The account of the queen's visit to Clare Hall on Wednesday 9 August, during her tour of the colleges, is brief: 'From her palace, she went first to Cleare hall where the master wayted with all his companye and receyvid her maiestie with an oracion' (which was delivered by John Welles).[40] From this statement, it is possible to imply that Nugent was indeed presented to the queen, perhaps in the manner in which she met processions of doctors and scholars at King's College during the previous weekend.[41]

Circumstantial collaborative evidence for their meeting may be adduced from the two commemorative volumes of poetry presented to the queen, which were requested from the colleges by William Cecil (chancellor of the university and Elizabeth's minister) in advance of the visit. This was a new departure for the university, but such institutional volumes had been presented on the occasion of previous royal visits by Edward VI to Winchester (1552) and by Elizabeth to Eton (1559/60 and 1563), while King's College in Cambridge (where Elizabeth stayed) also presented a separate volume to Elizabeth on the occasion of her 1564 visit.[42] Only one of the two volumes requested by Cecil survives, and it contains approximately 315 sets of verse (mostly in Latin) addressed to the queen. Contributions were grouped by collegial affiliation and within each section they were generally ordered by authors' seniority.[43] Nugent's position – fourth of 25 and ahead of some of the college's fellows, despite having matriculated a little over a year before – implies that he was near the top of the college social hierarchy.[44] This internal ranking suggests that if the queen was introduced to any of the members of Clare Hall on Wednesday 9 August, it is likely Nugent was among them. In contrast to her visit to Clare Hall, on her way north she did not delay long enough even to listen to the oration prepared for her visit to Magdalene College (the college of Nugent's Gaelic Irish contemporary and possible collaborator, Seaán Ó Cearnaigh), but made her excuses and requested that a written copy of the text be given to her instead.[45]

FLATTERING THE MONARCH

Nugent's gift of a manuscript might have appealed to Elizabeth on a number of personal levels. Between 1545 and 1548 she had presented handwritten copies of her own translations as New Year's gifts to her father, half-brother (Edward) and stepmother (Katherine Parr), and the surviving 1545 presentation copy of one such work (to Katherine Parr) is believed to have been bound by Elizabeth herself.[46] Indeed she took pleasure in her early calligraphic skills and regretted the deterioration of her penmanship as her life progressed.[47] Nugent's primer might have appealed to Elizabeth's codicological and handicraft tastes,[48] but, more importantly, his gift was undoubtedly intended to benefit from Elizabeth's intellectual curiosity and capitalize upon the great changes that had occurred both in the status of women and in female education during the previous half century.

At least superficially, much of Western Europe was being ruled by women in the 1560s: Elizabeth (queen of England), Mary Stewart (queen of Scots), Catherine de Medici (regent of France) and Margaret of Parma (regent of the Netherlands).[49] All these women had received superior and better-planned educations than the preceding generation of women, and nowhere was this more obvious than in England. Henry VIII's sisters had received a restricted schooling in comparison to him, but things had changed greatly by the time his daughters were being brought up, and the education of women was not only commended but also carefully planned. For example, Catherine of Aragon had commissioned the Spanish humanist Juan Luis Vives to draw up a detailed educational programme for the future Queen Mary.[50] Elizabeth, too, received a good humanist education; she was an assured Latinist and as at home in French and Italian as she was in English, although her grasp of Spanish (unlike Mary's) remained imperfect.[51] In contrast to Mary, Elizabeth became competent in Greek, having been taught by the great Cambridge scholar Roger Ascham.[52] Elizabeth's education, however advanced, was not career orientated; unlike her half-brother, Edward, she was not trained for government,[53] nor could she ever be considered a scholar monarch, comparable to her successor, James VI and I. Regardless of Elizabeth's level of intellectual attainment or its limitations, her youthful instruction certainly had a major influence on her life and future government policies; in particular she remained acutely conscious in adult life of how her education had shaped her religious outlook.[54] Consequently, Nugent's primer fitted into the tradition of presentation volumes mentioned above, which were not only commissioned by institutions but also by enterprising individuals who sought personal advancement, and it also spoke to increased humanist emphasis on female education (of which Elizabeth was a beneficiary).[55] It was designed to flatter Elizabeth by explicitly identifying her as a learned Renaissance prince, and offered reassurance that she could win over the recalcitrant Gaelic Irish by utilizing her proven capacity for learning foreign languages.[56] Despite ruling over one largely Gaelic-speaking kingdom and bordering another, Elizabeth had never sought instruction in Irish. This did not result from lack of opportunity (she was frequently surrounded by Irish-speaking courtiers, some among the very first rank of her favourites, such as her cousin 'Black Tom' Butler, earl of Ormond) – rather it was a consequence of the low standing of the Irish language (discussed in the next chapter).

NUGENT'S CAREER IN IRELAND

Although Nugent's Cambridge contemporaries might use their education as a stepping stone to a career in the law, church or at court, Nugent never lost sight of his native Delvin. Grants of lands in Laois and Offaly while he was still a student in Cambridge may suggest that he was already anxious to build his holding back home and that the establishment were keen that he would return.[57] Nugent turned 21 in the year following Elizabeth's visit (1565), thereby legally coming of age, and he left Cambridge towards the end of that year without taking a degree (a not uncommon occurrence) and returned to Ireland.[58] Before leaving he was apparently granted the lease of the abbey of All Saints and a captainship in Co. Longford.[59] On his return he sued for livery (the legal process for having his majority recognized) before Easter 1566 at a cost of £103 6s. 8¾d.,[60] and initially busied himself with consolidating his estates.[61] He was knighted by Lord Deputy Sidney in 1566 for his service against Shane O'Neill,[62] and Sidney also wrote to the privy council in January 1567 in support of suits by Nugent (of which Sidney claimed not to know the content, but felt obliged to commend Nugent to the privy council for his service in Ireland).[63] These suits may have been connected with Nugent's subsequent attempts to gain the leases of the ecclesiastical lands of Inchmore (Co. Longford) and Fore (Co. Westmeath) in March that year,[64] which Elizabeth granted that May.[65] This had the effect of placing considerable ecclesiastical patronage in the diocese of Kilmore into Nugent's hands.[66] It was also the last lease that Nugent was to receive, as his recusancy was becoming apparent.[67] The following month Shane O'Neill was killed and Nugent was present at the submission of his successor Turlough Luineach O'Neill to Lord Deputy Sidney,[68] which was famously illustrated in John Derrick's *The Image of Irelande, with a discouerie of Woodkarne*.[69]

Nugent's position was further strengthened by his marriage to Mary Fitzgerald, a daughter of the restored 11th earl of Kildare (the 'Wizard Earl'), and the subsequent matrimonial alliances of their 12 children (six boys and six girls) reinforced the Nugents' links with some of the most important families in Anglo-Irish and Gaelic Ireland, including Gaelic Irish nobles such as O'Brien of Thomond and O'Donnell of Tír Conaill, Anglo-Irish nobles like Fitzgerald of Kildare, and prominent gentry families of the Pale such as Cheevers of Co. Meath and Aylmer of Co. Kildare.[70] Despite a relatively prosperous first decade back in Ireland, Nugent fell foul of the Dublin government in 1574 for his refusal (ostensibly on procedural grounds) to sign a proclamation of rebellion against the earl of Desmond.[71] After some legal wrangling he submitted the following year and was restored to favour. More serious was his involvement in ongoing disputes over the 'cess', a relatively arbitrary system of taxation intended for the provisioning of the army, whose burden fell upon the Anglo-Irish landowners of the Pale, such as Nugent. The controversy rumbled on during the 1570s and Nugent's leading role in opposition to the cess had the twin effects of consolidating his standing among many of the Anglo-Irish nobility and gentry and alienating him from other members of the Dublin government.[72] More serious still was Viscount Baltinglass' rebellion (1580), in which Nugent did not directly participate but was implicated (not least because of the related rebellion of his brother, William).[73] Nugent – 'the shrewdest man in Leinster', according to his enemy Sir John Wallop[74] – and the earl of Kildare (his father-in-law) were imprisoned for 18 months, before being sent to England for further interrogation. He remained overseas in a relaxed form of custody until 1585, and curried favour with William Cecil (Lord Burghley), Elizabeth's minister and chancellor of his *alma mater*, who later promoted his admission as an honorary member of Gray's Inn (1588).[75]

On return to Ireland he attempted to lead a somewhat quieter life, largely in his native Delvin, but he became embroiled in conflict with Robert Dillon (chief justice of the common pleas), whom he accused of being responsible for the judicious murder of a kinsman and of obstructing various legal suits.[76] He launched an unsuccessful campaign to have Dillon convicted of treason, which also lead to antagonism with Lord Deputy Fitzwilliam, who was perhaps resentful that his jurisdiction was being circumscribed on the ground (north and west of Meath) by Nugent.[77] During the Nine Years War (1594–1603), Nugent was an active government military commander in the midlands and also involved in intelligence gathering (including translating intercepted letters of O'Neill into English). Despite his outward opposition to O'Neill and his allies, Nugent was held in suspicion because of his Catholicism, his previous associations, his occasional tacit support of the rebels, and the Tudor mistrust of bilinguals (particularly interpreters).[78] His surrender to O'Neill, after his lands became indefensible in 1599–1600, seemed to endorse the long-held suspicion in which he was held (despite the commission he received from the earl of Ormond to parley with O'Neill).[79] It was enough to destroy him and all his former services were soon forgotten; he was arrested in 1602 and died in prison in Dublin Castle later that year, before the government could put him on trial for treason.[80] He was buried at Castle Delvin (Clonyn, Co. Westmeath) and succeeded by his son, Richard (1583–1642), who was subsequently created earl of Westmeath (a title that survives to this day) and the Nugents emerged as one of the most important Catholic families in post-1603 Ireland.[81]

RETROSPECT

Christopher Nugent's life was not untypical of that of many of the Anglo-Irish community, who were required by necessity to negotiate a variety of political, social, cultural and religious environments simultaneously. The consequent demands on his loyalties that such an existence entailed, and the predicaments in which they embroiled him, have been admirably summarized by Colm Lennon:

> Christopher Nugent's case illustrates in a most acute form the dilemma of an older English resident of Ireland, caught up in the two cultures. His political loyalty was to the English establishment there, recently enhanced by the upgrading of the island's status to kingdom. His confessional allegiance to Rome was increasingly expressed in the form of open recusancy but in no way did it entail a transfer of fealty to the Roman Catholic enemies of England. He was a fervent upholder of the medieval Anglo-Norman constitution which enshrined the corporate rights of the colonial community in church and state. The thrust of religious and political reforms in the Elizabethan period threatened to override these rights of consultation and representation which Delvin had at heart. While resisting the diplomatic inducement of O'Neill during his rebellion, Delvin's close links with Gaelic society rendered him open to suspicion of collusion with the arch-traitor, and his antagonists in the Dublin administration seized the opportunity to disgrace him.[82]

However, in 1564 all of this was ahead of Christopher Nugent, and for the young man from Delvin the primer he presented to Elizabeth must have appeared to him to be a means of utilizing the century's changing linguistic attitudes (discussed in the next chapter) to his own advantage. It was to be an unfulfilled hope; his ability to move easily in and between the various cultural environments that enabled him to produce the primer also ultimately contributed to his undoing.

3. 'My speeche beinge Irishe is nott well understood': attitudes to Irish in the 16th century

Sixteenth-century Ireland was overwhelmingly Irish speaking and its history is in part the history of language.[1] As Patricia Palmer has noted, language in late-Tudor Ireland may be viewed in a variety of ways – from means of conciliation to fatal shibboleth – including:

> as medium of negotiation, as subject of interdictions, as badge of identity, as index of civility, as symbol of otherness, as bearer of ideology, as words in the mouth of a preacher, as battlecry, as lines tumbling off the newly established printing presses, as – when O'Donnell, on a hosting in Sligo, slaughtered all males unable to speak Irish – death-warrant.[2]

To these may be added – in the case of Christopher Nugent and his primer – as a vehicle for advancement. To consider his primer as a 'labour of love' and a product of the 'passionate advocacy of a hibernophile initiate' (as Palmer has) appears somewhat wide of the mark.[3] It was a document most likely crafted for personal gain that capitalized upon new and complex attitudes to language and language use (not just Irish), and this chapter will float the primer upon that tempestuous 16th-century linguistic sea, focusing on the place of the Irish language in practical politics and religious discourse.

LANGUAGE AND POLITICAL REFORM IN THE 16TH CENTURY

Since the suppression of the Kildare rebellion in the 1530s, the lord deputyship was held by a succession of men who did not speak Irish. Each was confronted and must have reflected (however superficially) on the issue of using Irish as a political and legal instrument, in a manner that would not have occurred to previous Anglo-Irish lords deputy, who were mostly fluent in Irish. Attitudes to Irish by the holders of this high office were as inconsistent and idiosyncratic as the men who held it, and each lord deputy in turn proceeded largely according to his own inclination. An example of how quickly things could change may be found in the careers of Thomas Radcliffe, 3rd earl of Sussex (Nugent's sometime guardian), and his successor, Sir Henry Sidney (by whom Nugent was knighted). In addition to Sussex's known linguistic abilities, he was sensible enough to realise the utility of having Irish speakers in his service, and his chaplain was described as a learned preacher in Irish (as noted above). Sussex envisioned a long reform process of anglicizing the Gaelic Irish and de-Gaelicizing the Anglo-Irish, in which political and legal flexibility would be required, during which he was willing to make certain compromises, such as displaying a willingness to use various aspects of brehon (Gaelic Irish) law when necessary. His successor, Sir Henry Sidney, was not so tolerant of brehon law, which he forbade for use in arbitration or other matters.[4] Of course the inclinations and ordinances of the lords deputy were of limited consequence in many parts of Gaelic Ireland, and frequently they were presented with the use of Irish for legal purposes as a *fait accompli*, as in September 1564 when a memorandum of agreement between Conor O'Brien (earl of Thomond) and his rival kinsman Sir Donal O'Brien was drawn up in Irish, and was only translated into English for Lord Deputy Sidney three years later.[5]

The 16th century did see some important (though by no means consistent) changes in English attitudes towards the Gaelic Irish and their language. One of the most notable departures was the temporarily successful (although ultimately failed) policy of 'surrender and regrant', which aimed to bring the Gaelic lordships into the political and cultural fold.[6] There were some successes, such as the gradual Anglicization and assimilation of the O'Briens of Thomond, but also patent failures, like the failed integration of the O'Neills of the north. When Shane O'Neill, perhaps the greatest Gaelic chief, visited Elizabeth's court at Whitehall in 1562, he expressed his otherness through language and dress. William Camden (writing almost half a century later) claimed that the costumes of Shane and his retinue were such that people stared at them in the kind of amazement Camden's own contemporaries would express upon seeing someone from China or America; hyperbole aside, it is likely that Shane's apparel was a deliberate political and cultural statement.[7] He had dressed in English style for part of his sojourn in England, and only reverted to his native apparel when formally meeting Elizabeth.[8] He 'performed' aspects of his Gaelic identity, through his costume and use of the Irish language, in order to support his assertions that he derived his authority and claim to the earldom of Tyrone from being 'Ó Néill', not from a gift of the monarch or by imitating English mannerisms. Furthermore, Shane delivered his submission orally in Irish, only later providing a written version in English, ostensibly because his speech in Irish would not be understood.[9] If Shane's speech was 'nott well understood', his point was well made and equally comprehended; it was certainly not to Cecil's liking, who objected to this flaunting of Gaelic culture in front of the queen.[10] Naturally, on occasion such sensibilities had to be overridden in the interests of pragmatism, as in the case of the 1541 Irish parliament that gave its consent to the act declaring Henry VIII king of Ireland. On that occasion a number of Gaelic Irish lords were invited to observe the proceedings (in the hope of making them more amenable to royal control) and James Butler, 9th earl of Ormond, translated some of the most important speeches into Irish for those visitors to the House of Lords.[11]

If Gaelic culture, particularly in its most blatant expression by Shane O'Neill, could seem antagonistic even in a submissive setting, then offering a means of accessing and neutralizing it through minimal engagement might prove beneficial to the recipient and vendor. As noted in the previous chapter, the primer's introduction suggested that Elizabeth could charm the Gaelic Irish through using their own language, and the six trilingual phrases (in Irish, Latin and English respectively) that Nugent supplied at the end of it were designed to do just that (being at their most basic level icebreakers intended to move conversation into a mutually intelligible language, specifically Latin).[12] The political climate that brought hitherto recalcitrant Gaelic Irish nobles like O'Neill and O'Brien into greater contact with the Dublin government and even with the English court made a guide to the Irish language like Nugent's seem an appropriate gift for the queen. The natural corollary was that the donor appeared more than just a supporter of government policy; he was advertising himself as a man with the linguistic and cultural wherewithal to implement it.

LANGUAGE AND RELIGIOUS REFORM IN THE 16TH CENTURY

Use of the Irish language (and language use in general) in 16th-century Ireland was further complicated by England's increasing Protestantism and Ireland's religious conservatism during this period, as issues of language use became increasingly associated with religious reform. Ultimately, Edwardian and Elizabethan desire to promote Protestantism and political reform reoriented the government's linguistic policy (such as it was) towards occasional acceptance of the Irish language in certain circumstances, to the end that the Gaelic population might be proselytized and integrated into the Tudor state.[13] Such partial changes ought not to be viewed in a narrow Irish context, but need to be understood in relation to evolving attitudes to other languages, including English.

The 16th century saw a widespread rise in the use of vernaculars as vehicles for learned and religious discourse throughout Europe and in this respect English was growing in prestige. While even as late as the 1530s English scholars could still question the utility of their own vernacular for religious discourse, the debate evolved during subsequent decades, from whether English could be used to discussions on the forms that should be used.[14] As Felicity Heal has pointed out, growing Tudor political centralism also 'nurtured a hegemonic view of [the English] language', which was demonstrated in the dedication of the government of Edward VI to disseminating Protestant texts in English during the late 1540s and early 1550s.[15] Since Englishmen had to make ideological and intellectual leaps to justify using their own vernacular in learned and religious discourse, it is unsurprising that they should prove slower to accept that the word of God should be translated into a vernacular they associated with a supposedly barbarous people. Nonetheless, there were calls for utilizing Irish in the promotion of the reformed religion; it may initially have been acceptable, from an English perspective, to promote preaching and catechizing in Irish, rather than jump straight to translating the liturgy and scripture.[16] Indeed the first book printed in the Irish language in Ireland was not the Bible, but a Protestant catechism: Seaán Ó Cearnaigh's *Aibidil Gaoidheilge & Caiticiosma* (1571), a work that will be shown to have close links with Nugent's primer.[17]

That which seems like linguistic toleration of a sort may ultimately have been intended as a stepping stone towards securing the hegemony of both English rule and the English language; the Irish language was to be the means of its own destruction. A parallel may be found in the contemporary translation of the Bible into Welsh, where a clause in the authorizing parliamentary statute of 1563 (the year Nugent matriculated at Cambridge) called for the English text to be placed alongside the Welsh translation, so that people 'might the sooner attain to the knowledge of the English tongue'.[18] Hiram Morgan has suggested that any supposed Elizabethan linguistic policy departure was 'gesture politics. It never formed part of a wider policy to respect Irish culture and language. If the Elizabethan state in Ireland had spent a tenth of what it spent on the materiel of war on bibles and prayer books in Irish and on an Irish-preaching clergy, history might have been different'.[19] It is hard to imagine any renaissance monarch spending the equivalent of 10 per cent of their military budget in this way, but Morgan is justifiably sceptical. Indeed, to speak of Tudor (or even Elizabethan) linguistic policy would be highly anachronistic and England's general Irish policy was characterized by what Ciaran Brady has called 'the periodic oscillations and simultaneous inconsistencies which were a feature of Tudor government in practice'.[20] Even though Edward and Elizabeth supported moves towards proselytizing in Irish and the production of Protestant printed material in Irish, the cause was not universally espoused. English was the preferred language of evangelization and efforts to provide religious literature in Irish were inconsistent and weak, with the 1560 Act of Uniformity preferring English and Latin over Irish for church use.[21] Lord Deputy St Ledger, who had first published the English-language *Book of Common Prayer* in Ireland in 1549, also received permission to print a Latin version.[22] A Latin translation (*Liber precum publicarum*) was published in 1560, ostensibly for those areas where English was not understood but was actually favoured within the English-speaking Pale, possibly because it preserved the more doctrinally conservative elements of the earlier (1549) prayer book (the English-language version had undergone subsequent revisions between 1549 and 1560).[23] Furthermore, preachers were also clearly hard to come by. When, in 1552, one candidate for an Irish benefice tried to excuse himself on the grounds that he did not speak Irish, Archbishop Cranmer declared in no uncertain terms, 'if he will take the pain to learn the Irish tongue (which with diligence he may do in a year or two) then both his person and doctrine shall be more acceptable not only unto his diocese, but also throughout all Ireland'.[24] A quarter of a century later things were little better, and in 1576 Lord Deputy Sidney wrote to Elizabeth asking her to write in turn to James Douglas, 4th earl of Morton (the Scottish regent), for Irish-speaking clergy to aid conversion.[25]

Ultimately, old habits die hard and Marc Caball's comments on the liturgy are applicable to the use of Irish in general: 'institutionally, a blend of suspicion and indifference characterized official attitudes to the use of Irish in the Anglican liturgy in the late sixteenth and early seventeenth centuries'.[26] Changes in official attitudes (or perhaps changes in the attitudes of officials) to the Irish language were not changes in perceptions of the intrinsic value of Irish, but in its perceived immediate utility, and toleration of Irish was a stepping-stone toward supplanting it with English. A similar attitude prevailed in the 17th century when, as Toby Barnard notes, the Church of Ireland occasionally compromised by using 'a language which it hoped would ultimately die out'.[27]

4. The medieval and Renaissance pedagogical contexts of the primer

Short as the primer is (only 9 folios/18 pages of text), it is significant in that it is one of the earliest (if not the earliest) extant documents in which an attempt is made to explain aspects of Irish grammar to a non-Irish speaking audience. Consequently, it ought to be accorded a prominent place in the history of Irish-language teaching; however, it has been almost universally ignored in this regard.[1] As with the approach adopted in the previous chapter (which sought to locate the primer within the political and religious linguistic climate of the 16th century), this chapter will seek to anchor it within a further 16th-century context, namely that of second language acquisition and pedagogy. In doing so, it will first highlight the long tradition of Irish grammatical analysis, then examine whether or not Nugent adopted/adapted an existing method for teaching Irish, before exploring the content of Nugent's linguistic education at the University of Cambridge and its Renaissance characteristics; finally, the relationship between Nugent's primer and Seaán Ó Cearnaigh's *Aibidil* (1571) is examined, as are possible connections between the two authors.

THE MEDIEVAL IRISH GRAMMATICAL TRADITION

The Irish had a long tradition of grammatical analysis in both the vernacular and Latin, as witnessed by texts such as the early 8th-century *Auraicept na nÉces* ('The scholar's primer'), whose authors applied the tools of classical grammatical analysis to the Irish language.[2] The *Auraicept* was a text held in high esteem, if not always utilized regularly, during the later Middle Ages,[3] during which time the main sources for Irish grammatical thought were the poetico-grammatical treatises written in Irish, produced by schools of Irish poets.[4] These poets were a learned elite occupying a privileged position in Gaelic society, who composed poems in praise of their aristocratic patrons for which they were rewarded richly. Their poetic compositions were written in accordance with strict linguistic conventions, in a type of Irish noticeably different from other contemporary forms, including spoken Irish. In the words of Damian McManus:

> Ní hionann an teanga sin agus teanga phróstéacsanna na linne; níorbh í gnáthchanúint duine ar bith, ná áit ar bith ná fiú tréimhse ar bith i stair na Gaeilge í. Caighdeán léannta tacair a bhí ann a bhí i bhfeidhm ar fud na tíre agus i nGaeltacht na hAlban.

(That language and the language of the prose texts of the time are not the same; it was not the vernacular of any person, nor any place nor even of any period in the history of Irish. Here was an artificial, learned standard, which was prevalent throughout the country and in the Gaelic-speaking area of Scotland.)[5]

These poetico-grammatical treatises were still being written in Nugent's lifetime, with one manuscript only dating about a decade before his primer.[6] As will be seen in the discussion of the contents of the primer (in the next chapter), a clear indebtedness to (though not precise agreement with) Irish bardic grammatical tradition may be observed in matters such as the names of letters, identification of diphthongs and triphthongs, and division of vowels and consonants.

Given the 'bad press' that Irish poets received from Elizabethans it was probably wise of Nugent not to highlight that his linguistic analysis derived from the bardic tradition.[7] Furthermore, aside from the language of instruction itself, other aspects of the contemporary bardic grammatical tracts were unsuitable for Nugent's purposes; for example, points in the grammatical tracts were illustrated with quotations from poetry, which would have been of little use to a beginner.[8] Instead he sought to give his pedagogical methods a more acceptable (and personally advantageous) pedigree, by associating them with his ancestor Elizabeth Zouche.

A FAMILY METHOD? ELIZABETH ZOUCHE (*ob.* 1517) AND WILLIAM BATHE (*ob.* 1614)

Seán Ó Mathúna has suggested that the methods employed in Nugent's primer were similar to those later used by his younger cousin, the Oxford-educated William Bathe SJ (of Drumcondra, Dublin), who published a Latin-Spanish primer entitled *Ianua linguarum* (1611), which subsequently became a popular tool for teaching Latin in the 17th century.[9] In the first edition of Bathe's *Ianua linguarum* the basic unit of instruction was a short, concise sentence, in Latin and Spanish, arranged in parallel columns, somewhat similar to f. 10v of Nugent's primer. Thus, to Ó Mathúna, two factors suggested a connection between Nugent's and Bathe's primers. First, a familial link; Nugent and Bathe were first cousins and, significantly, their maternal great-grandmother was Elizabeth Zouche, whom Nugent claimed was taught Irish in the manner he prescribed. Secondly, a structural link; both Nugent and Bathe employed parallel sentences in Latin and the vernacular.

In fact, aside from the parallel sentences (of which there are only six in Nugent's work), there is little to link the two primers. By way of contrast it might be noted that, unlike Nugent, Bathe did not make any mention of Zouche or the origin of his methods, he did not discuss linguistic features, analyse orthography or phonology, nor did he alter orthography in the manner that Nugent did for pronunciation purposes. Ó Mathúna went to considerable length to place Bathe's *Ianua linguarum* within the wider European educational context, while simultaneously (and almost casually) suggesting that Bathe's bilingual approach was based on the method used to teach Elizabeth Zouche, which is otherwise only attested in Nugent's primer.[10] But as Ó Mathúna also notes, some grammars of the first half of the 16th century already employed a bilingual approach, such as William Lily's *A shorte introduction of grammar* (*c.*1513), while *colloquia*, like Seybaldus Hayden's *Formulae puerilium colloquiorum* (1530), also utilized a short sentence method; both of which predate our primers.[11] To these examples may be added the works of William Horman, who taught at Eton and was the author of an introduction to Latin; in 1519 he published a large collection of *vulgaria* (English sentences with model Latin translations).[12] A detailed investigation would doubtless uncover more examples. Unfortunately, the limited lexicon of Nugent's primer and our ignorance of any further details concerning Elizabeth Zouche's instruction in Irish severely restricts the amount of material available for comparative purposes, but overall there does not seem to be any solid basis for seeing a link between Nugent's and Bathe's works.

In the preface Nugent claims that 'it pleasyde your maiestie (which I take aspetiall fauor) to comaunde me delyuer your Highnes the Iryshe Caracters with instructions for reading of the language', which ostensibly suggests that he was asked to produce a guide to reading (and not necessarily speaking) Irish.[13] This may relate to his statement that:

> For commonlye men do learne by demaundinge the signyfacation of the wordes, not by the letter, as your Maiestie hath here sett downe vnto you, which is the spedyer, and better way; in profe whereof (men yett lyuinge which knewe Elizabethe zouche, daughter to the Lorde Zouch, sometime Countesse of kyldare, Do affirme that in shorte tyme she learned to reade, write, and perfectlye speake the tongue.[14]

The method by which Elizabeth Zouche was taught Irish and how closely it correlated to Nugent's primer is unknowable, and indeed Nugent may have had no knowledge of how the countess was introduced to Irish. He may simply have been name-dropping; Elizabeth Zouche – wife of the 9th earl of Kildare and Nugent's great-grandmother – was the closest familial connection Nugent had to the Tudors. In 1503 Gearóid Óg Fitzgerald (future 9th earl) married Elizabeth, daughter of Sir John Zouche of Codnor, Derbyshire, cousin of Henry VII, and the king and Gearóid's father (the 8th earl) granted them lands in England and Ireland.[15] She was the mother of Silken Thomas and four girls, and died unexpectedly at Lucan in 1517.

Regardless of the veracity of his assertion (or lack thereof), Nugent claims to have provided the queen with a means of learning Irish 'by the letter' (which he considered preferable), rather than by 'the signyfacation of the wordes'. Recently, Pádraig Ó Macháin has suggested that this means learning Irish through the written word, rather than the spoken word, and while this is a possibility, I am unaware of the use of the word 'signyfacation' to imply 'enunciation', as opposed to the standard 'meaning'. It is possible that 'by the letter' means 'through grammatical analysis', whereas someone learning by the 'signyfacation of the wordes' learns stores of vocabulary, their regular meanings, and possibly their etymologies/metaphysical meanings. If this interpretation is correct, it may explain why Nugent devotes over twice as much space to such grammatical analysis (ff 6r–9r) as to vocabulary and sample sentences (ff 9v–10v). This would actually place his methods in direct contrast to those of his first cousin, William Bathe, who advocated learning large stores of vocabulary through his sample sentences, in which grammar would be casually acquired.[16]

RENAISSANCE SECOND-LANGUAGE TEACHING AND THE POSSIBLE IMPACT OF NUGENT'S CAMBRIDGE EDUCATION ON THE PRIMER

If Nugent did compose the primer after meeting Elizabeth in 1564 and before he returned to Ireland in 1565, then it is quite possible that his time at Cambridge influenced its conception and construction. When searching for influences on Nugent (or Bathe or Ó Cearnaigh), it should be noted that Europe in the century prior to their works saw intense speculation on educational methods, notably in the field of language teaching and especially in the case of second-language acquisition.[17] Humanist attempts to acquire Greek in the 15th century may have been the stimulus for teachers to re-examine traditional grammatical doctrine and teaching methods.[18] Educational theory has rarely had so strong an influence on practical teaching as it did during the 16th century, and it occupied the minds of great thinkers like the Dutch humanist Desiderius Erasmus (1466–1536) and the prolific Spanish educator Juan Luis Vives (1492–1540).[19]

Nugent and Ó Cearnaigh attended Cambridge, and Bathe went to Oxford, at a period when these universities were home to considerable philosophical and pedagogical controversy over modes of memorization, which had implications for methods of language teaching, most notably between the followers of the Italian philosopher Giordano Bruno (1548–1600) and those of the French humanist Pierre de la Ramée (Peter Ramus, 1515–72), and Ramism was particularly popular in Cambridge into the first decades of the 17th century.[20] Renaissance influences may be seen in the physical layout of information on Nugent's pages (such as his methods of bracketing information), which imitates standard contemporary printed grammars, while the nested diagrammatic forms used by Nugent's Cambridge contemporary, Ó Cearnaigh, are quintessentially Ramian.[21] These stand in contrast to the less visually differentiated layout in Irish bardic manuscripts – regardless of what content Nugent and Ó Cearnaigh derived or did not derive from the medieval Irish tradition, they packaged it in a format imitative of early modern printed works. Unfortunately, owing to a dearth of information on Nugent's university days (including what he might have been taught, who taught him, and what books he read), the best that can be done to investigate the influences that may have acted upon him is to approach the topic sideways, by looking at the general curriculum of the university and the reading habits of his contemporaries.

Beginning with the curriculum, we find that the university's syllabus was vague and subject to repeated tinkering, often owing to the religious and intellectual inclinations of the monarchs; Henry, Edward, Mary and Elizabeth all engaged in varying degrees of prescribing and proscribing. The statutes of the University of Cambridge – as indicators of curriculum content – have to be treated with caution, for as Elisabeth Leedham-Green has noted of the Elizabethan statutes of 1570:

> Here, as with the earlier statutory regulations for the curriculum, we may see with what caution such regulations should be interpreted. Where, as so often, they merely codified existing practice, they serve as mileposts rather than signposts; when they attempted a radical reform they were commonly ignored.[22]

Overall the curriculum shifts in arts between *c.*1450 and *c.*1600 saw 'a move away from formal logic and modal grammar to literature, rhetoric and some arithmetic for undergraduates, from further logic and Aristotelian natural and moral philosophy to a more widely based natural and moral philosophy for BAs'.[23] The curriculum of Nugent's time was probably in essence that prescribed during the reign of Edward VI, yet it was a general outline of what each year's study should contain and not a detailed syllabus.[24] Indeed, it has been suggested that the statutes were deliberately left vague, in order to avoid narrowly restricting tutors or students.[25] The implementation of these guidelines was very much at the discretion of individual tutors and it was probably at the level of individual tutor-student interaction that the most profound educational influence was to be felt.[26] Tutors were usually chosen according to the educational and religious preferences of students' parents. Unfortunately, the name of Nugent's tutor is not known, but it is possible that Nugent's linguistically accomplished guardian, the earl of Sussex (who was competent in English, Latin, Italian and perhaps Spanish), would have had him placed under the instruction of a suitably minded tutor.[27]

Broadly speaking the subjects of the trivium (grammar, rhetoric and dialectic or logic) were those upon which an undergraduate degree was based, and were concerned with language and its effective use in rational argument.[28] Not all of them would have been studied at the same time, and the Elizabethan statutes (1570) prescribed rhetoric for year one, dialectic for years two and three, and philosophy for year four.[29] In terms of dialectic (which Nugent might have

studied in year two), John Seton's short manual, *Dialectica* (first published in
1545), was the main set text from about 1560 onwards, but Ramus was also
extremely popular with students:[30] when the Cambridge-based bookseller John
Denys died in the late 1570s he had 22 different editions of Ramus' writings in
his possession.[31] Pádraig Ó Macháin has suggested that Nugent's grammatical
discussion is based upon the teaching of the classical scholar Aelius Donatus,
who was still popular into the Renaissance period.[32] Given Nugent's ability to
compose a section of the primer in Latin, it is possible that he may have been
familiar with Donatus before travelling to England. Overall, considering the
short time period Nugent spent at Cambridge, the amount he absorbed from
formal teaching may have been limited.

Aside from what he might have been taught, it is also difficult to know what
else a student like Nugent might have read at Cambridge. Religious upheavals
sometimes saw the purging of libraries in the universities, hampering attempts
even at identifying holdings at a given time.[33] Furthermore, college libraries did
not loan books easily; book borrowing was a formal process that occurred at
specific times and places, meaning that Nugent may not have had casual access
to whatever was on the shelves.[34] However, college fellows' personal libraries
may have been intended for student use, as suggested by multiple copies of the
same work in individual postmortem book inventories,[35] and might provide a
more promising avenue of enquiry. With regard to what might have been read
at Clare Hall, only one book inventory for an exact contemporary of Nugent's
survives, that of John Welles, who was a fellow in 1564–5 and who delivered the
oration to Elizabeth in 1564.[36] That inventory dates, however, from Welles' death
in 1569/70, and it cannot be ascertained how many of the books he owned at the
time of his demise were already in his possession while both he and Nugent
were at Clare Hall.[37] Among the 16th-century grammatical works in Welles'
possession were an unnamed Greek lexicon/dictionary, a copy of *Calapinus*
(presumably the *Dictionarium* of the Italian lexicographer Ambrosius Calepinus)
and a *Grammatica Cleonardi Greca* (possibly one of the two textbooks for students
of Greek, written by the Flemish grammarian, Nicolaas Cleynaerts). He also
possessed a number of books on rhetoric and over ten volumes of Cicero (some
of whose works were generally set texts for teaching rhetoric).[38] Although it
is unknowable whether Welles may have granted Nugent access to his library,
possible grounds for rapport between Welles and Nugent may have been their
Catholicism (or at least Welles' Catholic sympathies), as suggested by Welles'
possession of a Roman breviary and his complaints of Calvinism in St John's
College.[39]

NUGENT AND Ó CEARNAIGH: ANGLO-IRISH CATHOLIC FELLOW COMMONER VERSUS GAELIC IRISH PROTESTANT SIZAR

It is possible that the strongest influence (broadly defined) upon Nugent's primer was Seaán Ó Cearnaigh, an exact contemporary of his at Cambridge. Ó Cearnaigh matriculated in 1561 and took his BA in 1565, while Nugent matriculated in 1563 and also left in 1565.[40] In an address to the reader at the beginning of his 1571 book *Aibidil Gaoidheilge & Caiticiosma*, Ó Cearnaigh makes mention of a version he prepared in 1563, while both he and Nugent were at Cambridge. Nicholas Williams raised the possibility that Ó Cearnaigh circulated his material in manuscript form first, for the opinion of fellow Irishmen at Cambridge.[41] Likewise, Pádraig Ó Macháin, while non-committal about the primer's production for Elizabeth's visit, has questioned whether the material on ff 8r–10v might have been based upon Ó Cearnaigh's earlier draft of the material that subsequently featured in *Aibidil*.[42] Could they have known each other in Cambridge? Is it possible that Ó Cearnaigh and Nugent shared work and ideas? Indeed is it possible that Nugent plagiarized his acquaintance's work? We will likely never know, but the arrangement of both primers into alphabet, letter classification and 'diphthong' classification, and the internal similarities within them (such as the identical ordering of the 17 diphthongs), all strongly suggests more than just a casual relationship.[43] Even stronger evidence may be found in the innovative material shared by the two, such as the neologism *collailm* (the name for the letter 'k')[44] and – as Ó Macháin has noted – the earliest written example of the relative particle *a*, which occurs in the primer and is next attested in Ó Cearnaigh's *Aibidil*.[45]

If the similarities between Nugent's and Ó Cearnaigh's work were the result of their acquaintance, what might have been the nature of their relationship? It would be somewhat anachronistic to suppose that they banded together out of a sense of common nationality. Ostensibly, Nugent was Anglo-Irish, while Ó Cearnaigh was Gaelic Irish and the religious differences between the Catholic Nugent and Protestant Ó Cearnaigh might also have kept them apart. Equally important may have been the gulf between their respective social statuses. The university was not a solvent for social bonds but a place where students honed their appreciation of the importance of social stratification, albeit at close quarters. The manner of Nugent's and Ó Cearnaigh's individual matriculations would have further solidified social differentiation. In tandem with academic instruction, students also acquired an informal social and political education at the university; future patrons and future clients rubbed shoulders as students, each learning to manipulate the norms of Tudor patronage. Aristocratic students learned the leadership skills necessary to construct webs of associations and dependents of the type that would be essential for a successful career as a country gentleman or courtier; poorer students learned how to cultivate, impress and ingratiate themselves with wealthy patrons.[46] Indeed, tutors too played the patronage game, in the hope of future reward after they had left their fellowships, or to bolster their positions in internal collegiate faction struggles.[47]

Ó Cearnaigh matriculated as a sizar at Magdalene College, a new and particularly poor institution, where the vast majority of students were sizars and pensioners, looking to progress through education.[48] In contrast, Nugent was a fellow commoner of Clare Hall, one of the oldest colleges in Cambridge. Fellow commoners paid the highest fees and were privileged in a variety of ways, including certain examination exemptions and the right to dine at high table with the college fellows.[49] Sizars, however, were at the bottom of the collegiate ladder and financed their studies by performing servants' tasks, such as cleaning the courts or waiting upon the fellows and fellow commoners at table in the dining halls.[50] Thus the differences between Ó Cearnaigh and Nugent existed at ancestral, financial, religious, collegial and social levels, the latter having separate Irish and Cambridge manifestations. Although there is circumstantial evidence for a relationship between their two documents, it is not possible to say whether this was the result of collaboration; there is certainly nothing to suggest any contact between the two authors after 1565.

CONCLUSION

Nugent's primer somewhat vaguely reflected the spirit of an age when second-language teaching was a matter of great intellectual importance, but it does not seem possible at this juncture to identify how far his Cambridge education or circumstances may have influenced it. In terms of the inspiration for its structure and content, the question of the extent to which it derived from a method used to teach Irish to Elizabeth Zouche in the first decade of the 16th century is ultimately unanswerable, and may well be a red herring. Considering the similarities between the primer and Ó Cearnaigh's *Aibidil* it seems more likely that Nugent may have borrowed from Ó Cearnaigh's pre-publication work, than from a putative 'family' method, or from William Bathe's *Ianua linguarum*.

5. The primer's contents

The aim of this chapter is to provide a brief analysis of each section of Nugent's primer, which has not been systematically undertaken in print before. The contents have been divided as follows:

1r–1v	[blank]
2r–4v	Dedication (in English)
5r–7v	'Originall of the nation' (in Latin)
8r	Alphabet
8v	Vowels and consonants
9r	Diphthongs
9v–10r	Word list (12 items)
10v	Phrase list (6 items)
11r–12v	[blank]

BINDING

The primer's limp vellum binding may have been the work of John Denys, who worked frequently for the University of Cambridge, and in whose probate inventory a gilding press is recorded, although two other binders (David Pearson and 'Philip Stacyoner') could also be candidates.[1] There are similarities between the bindings of Nugent's primer and the surviving volume of verse presented to Elizabeth in 1564. Both have cream-coloured limp vellum bindings that would have originally been tied shut with silk thread (gold in the primer, green in the verse volume).[2] Interestingly, the verse volume was described by a contemporary as 'bound in a parchment coverynge, gylt with flouris of gold at the four corners, knit with green ribband string'.[3] Elisabeth Leedham Green notes that the present binding of the verse volume is probably contemporary, and clearly has no gilt flowers. It is stamped front and back with ELIZABETHA REGINA within a crude asymmetrical frame that also contains a crown and leopard, and a separate gilt oval centrepiece.[4] The contemporary description seems less than accurate, and it actually better describes the primer's binding; it may be that it refers to the lost companion volume of verse, which may have been bound similarly to the primer. Overall, both bindings were somewhat amateurish, that of the primer slightly less so.

1r–1v AND 11r–12v (BLANK)

While normally blank leaves at the beginning and end of a volume are believed to act as flyleaves (inserted by binders to protect the outer text leaves from damage), Renaissance text books were deliberately furnished with blank leaves to be filled in by the student in a manner that they found appropriate.[5] It is perhaps more surprising that the book lacks a title page, which under normal circumstances would have been used to advertise the constituent parts of the book; however, given that the primer was not intended for publication, this sort of marketing information may not have been deemed necessary.[6]

2r–4v: DEDICATION (IN ENGLISH)

Dedications such as the one occupying ff 2r–4v were frequently used to highlight a special relationship between the author and dedicatee (or a desire for one). Although there is no independent evidence to corroborate Nugent's claim in the dedication that Elizabeth requested the primer, it would be highly bizarre for Nugent to falsely claim she did so.[7] If Elizabeth commissioned the primer (whether casually or with serious intent), she may have done so as a form of royal image fashioning – to be seen to make the request was more important than desiring or using it.[8] Regardless, Nugent began his work by framing it along the lines of other early modern 'how-to' books, which were grounded in the experience of their authors and positioned their readers as actors, offering them a means of assuming new forms of authority and transforming their identity through knowledge acquisition.[9] The introduction advises Elizabeth on the benefits that she and Ireland will gain through her acquisition of the Irish language, including increased Gaelic-Irish obedience, justice, civility and affection for the monarch – framing it as a confessionally ambiguous 'holy intent' – while she in turn will leave an example of virtue for posterity, outstripping that of her predecessors (there is also the hint to the ever-parsimonious Elizabeth that this path will turn out cheaper in the long run). Nugent promises that neither the language nor the methods he advocates for learning it are particularly difficult, and especially not for someone of Elizabeth's renowned linguistic capabilities, thus counteracting the position of the Irish language as 'yet another element in the Elizabethans' dystopic assessment of Gaelic Ireland'.[10] His approach also places the dedication within standard contemporary practice, in which 'prefaces to the general reader or to a specific patron guided use by highlighting or theorizing the social significance and methodological stakes of the topic. Furthermore, they offered the opportunity for presenting a version of the reader to himself or herself, as a patron worthy to be flattered, or as one of those capable of being educated'.[11]

The methods Nugent advocates were those he claimed were used to teach Irish to Elizabeth Zouche, who married the 9th earl of Kildare, and was a kinswoman of Margaret Beaufort, mother of Henry VII.[12] A catalogue of the library of the 9th earl of Kildare indicates that the earl possessed a number of grammatical works in Latin (including Ambrosius Calepinus' *Dictionarium*, a copy of which was possessed by Nugent's Clare Hall contemporary John Welles), but none in Irish.[13] If, as Nugent claimed, his method of teaching Irish 'by the letter' (through studying grammar) was practised in the Fitzgerald household, then it is curious that the libraries of Zouche's husband and father-in-law did not contain any works that could have been used for her instruction. As previously alluded to, Nugent may have been name-dropping on this occasion, as Elizabeth Zouche was his great-grandmother and his closest blood link to the Tudors.

As noted in the first chapter, Nugent emphasized his Englishness by framing the Gaelic Irish as 'other'. It was expedient for Nugent to stress his Englishness given the occasional cultural ignorance that Anglo-Irish nobles experienced in England – two years previously, Christopher St Lawrence, 7th Baron Howth, had been sent to Elizabeth's court to defend Lord Deputy Sussex's campaigns only to find himself questioned by Elizabeth whether he 'could speak the English tongue'.[14] Consequently, whereas Ó Cearnaigh repeatedly speaks inclusively in the first person plural in *Aibidil*, Nugent does not, as Ó Cearnaigh had a fellow Gaelic Irish audience in mind, while Nugent needed to stress to his audience (that is Elizabeth) that he was English. Likewise, in deferring to the linguistic authority of the bardic schools Ó Cearnaigh was engaging in a form of Gaelic Irish cultural solidarity in which Nugent could never indulge, owing to the politically poisonous position of the bards in the Elizabethan English mindset.[15] More curious, however, is that Ó Cearnaigh acknowledges Elizabeth as queen in an Irish context, whereas Nugent later used the phrase 'Queene off Englande'.[16]

The dedication is written in a fine Renaissance book-hand and begins with a woodcut-like initial 'A', which (like the 'C' on f. 5r) Pádraig Ó Macháin has suggested was drawn by hand.[17] The signature appears to be that of Christopher Nugent, and is written in lighter ink in a slightly cursive hand, and it is possible (though uncertain) that he is the scribe of the entire manuscript.[18] If not, then Nugent may have commissioned a professional scribe (or perhaps even Ó Cearnaigh?) to execute it and then appended his own name to it. It is interesting that Nugent signs himself as a peer, '.C. Deluín' (Christopher Delvin), rather than by his family name, perhaps to advertise the imminent termination of his minority and a desire to return to Ireland.

5r–7v: 'originall of the nation' (in latin)

Like the preceding section, this one does not have a title, but I have adopted the term 'Originall of the nation', as Nugent used this phrase in the Dedication to describe an unasked-for section that he thought necessary to include 'to the ende your maiestye knowinge from whence they came, & theire tongue deryued,

might the soner attaine to the perfection thereof'.[19] To signify the importance
of this unrequested 'Originall of the nation' he employs Latin, the language of
scholarly disputation and high culture. It starts with an historical background
to the Gaelic Irish people and the Irish language, which begins in the time of
'Phaleg' (Peleg) and the initial division of the world (Genesis 10:25), explaining
how the Irish-speaking peoples (including those of Scotland, the Hebrides and
the Isle of Man) descend from Gaedhelus, five generations posterior to Iaphet,
son of Noah.[20] This material is ultimately based upon the aetiological traditions
of *Lebor gabála Érenn* (The book of the taking of Ireland), but the 'Originall
of the nation' explicitly cites book 3, chapter 7 of Gerald of Wales' (Giraldus
Cambrensis') *Topographia Hibernica* (Topography of Ireland).[21] At this period the
writings of Gerald, although widely known, had not yet been published,[22] and
regardless of what version of the *Topographia* Nugent had access to (presumably
in Cambridge), he expected Elizabeth to have access to a copy too (or at least
a familiarity with the text).[23] Nugent's use of Gerald may be placed within a
tradition of reading Gerald in medieval Ireland, in which Anglo-Irish families
like the Fitzgeralds used the *Topographia* and Gerald's *Expugnatio Hibernica*
(Conquest of Ireland) as quasi-origin legends for their families and their own
right to rule (dovetailing nicely with the Gaelic origin legend), rather than as a
means of justifying the later Tudor conquest.[24] Thus, Nugent's approach speaks
to an Anglo-Irish outlook that predates the various schools of Catholic and
Protestant historiography (and their complicated relationships with Gerald) that
developed from the late 16th century and flourished in the first half of the 17th
century.[25]

    The core of this section involves highlighting correspondences between Irish
and the Three Sacred Languages (Hebrew, Greek and Latin), using the teachings
of the classical grammarian Donatus, and illustrated with selected examples.[26] It
focuses in particular on metaplasmus (alteration of a word by adding, omitting
or transporting sounds or syllables) and aspiration (pronouncing a sound with
an exhalation of breath). For example, Nugent observes that the Irish uses
the Greek *aspir* symbol (represented in this transcription as **h**) and that for the
words for 'father' and 'mother' *in latina locutione vocem, pater, mutauit in at**h**air seu
athair, sonans, aher. p, Aphæresicôs reiecta. Mater, verti in mat**h**ir sonans, maher* ('in
Latin speech *pater* is changed into *at**h**air* or *athair*, pronounced *aher*, p is rejected
through aphaeresis.[27] *Mater*, is changed into *mat**h**air*, pronounced *maher*').[28]
Nugent also uses Hebrew and Greek examples, his knowledge of which may
have been acquired in Cambridge. If so, referring to the pronunciation of Greek
was a flirtation with danger. In 1542 and 1543 Bishop Stephen Gardiner, who
succeeded Thomas Cromwell as chancellor of the university, banned the new
pronunciation of Greek that had been advocated by Thomas Smith (Regius
Professor of Civil Law) and John Cheke (Regius Professor of Greek).[29] The
debate over the two modes of pronunciation was ideological in nature and
highly self-conscious.[30]

Comparing a vernacular with Hebrew, Greek and Latin would not have seemed out of place to Elizabeth, even if she did not know that this was already a commonplace in Irish grammatical tradition from the early medieval period. The elevation of a vernacular to a place of pre-eminence alongside the Sacred Languages was a trope with which Elizabeth was probably already familiar. William Tyndale, the reformer and translator of the bible, claimed that English had a natural affinity with Greek and Hebrew and that 'the properties of the Hebrew tongue agreeth a thousand times more with English than with the Latin'.[31] Similarly, William Salesbury, in his 1550 volume on Welsh pronunciation, claimed of Welsh that 'the Brytyshe tonge hath [language] as commune, yea, rather as peculiar or sisterlyke with the holy language, the Hebrewe tonge'.[32] This type of linguistic speculation was related to the search for the primal tongue spoken before the Fall – which could be used to overcome religious differences – and continued during the course of the 16th and 17th centuries.[33]

8r: ALPHABET

The alphabet page begins with 'The Irish Alphabet' written in a gothic hand,[34] followed by a letter-only version of the alphabet in two lines, and a second version in a table that includes the *ogam* names of the letters, both of which versions follow the Latin alphabetical sequence (a, b, c, etc.), and which for convenience's sake will be referred to as the linear alphabet and the tabular alphabet respectively. The ordering of the letters according to the Latin alphabet (as opposed to the *ogam* alphabet) may seem an obvious choice for a work being presented to someone with no background in Irish, but it was to become also the standard ordering in Irish discussions too.[35]

The *Aibidil* likewise contains an alphabet page, and, similar to Nugent's linear-alphabet ending in 'amen', Ó Cearnaigh's alphabet is preceded by a Trinitarian invocation, also ending in 'amen'.[36] Ó Cearnaigh's overall format was hardly innovative, as the idea of combining the alphabet with an official short catechism may be seen in the standard English work, *The ABC with the catechism*, which was printed in the tens of thousands during every decade of Elizabeth's reign.[37] Thus Ó Cearnaigh's alphabet page shows an indebtedness to 16th-century prayer books, which often consisted of several leaves with basic prayers in English or Latin, beginning with an alphabet in those that were intended to act as teaching guides for reading and writing.[38] In the 16th century, Protestants and Catholics alike linked acquisition of literacy (both reading and writing) to teaching the basics of religion,[39] and the 'amen' of Nugent's linear alphabet seems a relict of this practice; its chiming with the 'holy intent' of the dedication probably accidental.

Looking at the linear alphabet, initially it appears more surprising for its additions, namely the inclusion of the letters 'k', 'q', 'v' 'x' and 'y', which do not normally feature in Irish orthography, than for its omissions ('j', 'w' and 'z'). Obviously any numerate Irish speaker would have been familiar with 'x' and 'v' (which doubled as Roman numerals), while the inclusion of 'q' is less surprising if we take into account that it is also found in the late medieval *ogam* manuscript tradition. In that scholastic *ogam* tradition, 'q' was designated by the name *ceart*.[40] The 'v' may actually be an angular form of 'u'; it does not feature independently in the primer and only ever appears in the form of 'v' + subscript 'i' (for 'ui'). The 'y' in the linear alphabet might actually be the backward 'c' representing 'con-', which would link it further to Ó Cearnaigh's alphabet and also means that there is less discrepancy between the linear and tabular alphabets (and would also explain why 'y' is not in the following folio on vowels and consonants). After the letters proper are the compendia 'v' + subscript 'i' (for 'ui'), the *Tironian notum* '7' (for *agus* 'and'), and the *et* ('and') ligature. Likewise, Ó Cearnaigh includes a brief note on each of these.[41]

Turning to the tabular alphabet, we find that the letters have been supplied with their Irish names, which derive from the *ogam* tradition and were the names by which letters were referred in the late medieval bardic grammatical treatises. In classical learning, letter names had a 'memno-technical' purpose, as the memorizing of letter names in the correct order was the first step in linguistic instruction.[42] Unlike their Latin or Greek counterparts (*A/Alpha*, *Be/Beta*, etc.), these Irish letter names are all meaningful words (many are the names of trees), and generally follow an acrostic principle.[43] The table is divided into two groups of three columns each for letters 'a'–'k' and 'l'–'u' respectively, with each entry consisting of Gaelic letter + *ogam* name + lower-case gothic letter.

In contrast to the linear alphabet, 'v', 'x' and 'y' (if such it is) are absent from the tabular alphabet. Other anomalies/inconsistencies include two uses of the tall form of 'e' in the tabular alphabet (in the names *fearn* ('f') and *ceart* ('q')) possibly to denote 'ea', although Nugent neither includes a tall 'e' in his linear alphabet nor explains this convention (if such it is), and it does not appear elsewhere in the primer.[44] Among the letter names it may be noted that Nugent calls 'p' *peth*, in contrast to the more usual *pethbog* (as found in Ó Cearnaigh's *Aibidil* and later Ó hEódhasa's grammar),[45] and excludes 'z' *straiph*.[46] An interesting point of overlap between Nugent's and Ó Cearnaigh's primers may be seen in the *ogam* name given to 'k' in both.[47] In his *Aibidil*, Ó Cearnaigh explains that *k. áchd gidh áinmníghtheár ann sa n-aibidil é, ní goirthear guthaighí nā consoin de. 7 gídheadh cuirthear a n-ionad. c, a, hé go meníoch* ('k: however, though it is listed in the alphabet is not named as a vowel or consonant; nevertheless it is frequently used to represent *ca*').[48] The name for 'k' (*collailm*) is a combination of the names for 'c' (*coll*) and 'a' (*ailm*) and Ó Cearnaigh's modern editor, Brian Ó Cuív, suggests that this name was an innovation (presumably on Ó Cearnaigh's part).[49] Ó Cuív, however, does not appear to have taken Nugent's primer into account in his work on Ó Cearnaigh.[50] It is unlikely that Nugent was responsible for the neologism; at no point did he require a 'k' (except in the subsequent page

on vowels and consonants) and therefore there appears little reason for him to
have coined an *ogam* name for it.

8v: VOWELS AND CONSONANTS

Following on from his alphabets, Nugent discusses the vowels and consonants.
He notes that there are five vowels, which he divides into 'a', 'o' and 'u'
('Soundinge broad & long') and 'e' and 'i' ('soundynge shorte & sharp'). The
consonants are 'b', 'd', 'g', 'l', 'm', 'n' and 'r' ('in pronuntiation, lyght and
shorte') and 'c', 'f', 'k', 'p', 'q', 's' and 't' ('in pronuntiation, heauye and longe').
Notwithstanding that all vowels may be long or short, and consonants may
be neither, it appears that he has divided his alphabet into broad vowels ('a',
'o', 'u'), slender vowels ('e' and 'i'), followed by liquid consonants and voiced
plosives ('b', 'd', 'g', 'l', 'm', 'n' and 'r'), and voiceless plosives, the fricative 'f'
and sibilant 's' ('c', 'f', 'k', 'p', 'q', 's' and 't').[51] Unfortunately, since Nugent
has alphabetized the ordering of the letters in each of his four categories, it is
difficult to say anything about his understanding of the internal divisions of his
groupings.[52] Overall, while his divisions are not without foundation, they bear
a limited correspondence to the bardic grammatical traditions, and Ó Macháin
has suggested that Nugent may have eschewed traditional methods 'in favour of
a less pedantic analysis'.[53] Nugent makes no provision for 'v', 'x' or 'y', which
are variously included in the alphabetical lists, nor for 'h', which is significant in
light of his discussion of aspiration in the 'Originall of the nation'.

9r: DIPHTHONGS

Progressing from his discussion of individual letters, Nugent claims that there
are 17 diphthongs in Irish, which he lists but on which he offers no comment.
It cannot be a coincidence that these are also listed, in exactly the same order,
in Ó Cearnaigh's corresponding table. Irish does not possess 17 diphthongs
and it appears – following Brian Ó Cuív's analysis of the corresponding list
in *Aibidil* – that these 17 forms represent a combination of six diphthongs, five
of those diphthongs with an additional vowel to indicate the palatalization
of the following consonant, and six digraphs.[54] Unlike Nugent, Ó Cearnaigh
subdivided the diphthongs and the indebtedness of these divisions to Irish
grammatical tradition is implied by his use of the names applied to these
categories in the poetical grammatical tracts, which are also included in the
Rudimenta grammaticae Hibernicae of Giolla Brighde Ó hEódhasa (*ob.* 1614),
the poet turned Franciscan who was educated alongside Nugent's brother,
William. Giolla Brighde (or Bonaventura as he became known on entering the
Franciscans) also identified 17 vowel combinations, which he divided into 12

diphthongs and five triphthongs and which match those found in Nugent's and Ó Cearnaigh's tables.[55]

Nugent then progressed to providing Elizabeth with a trilingual word list, containing only 12 examples. These were arranged six to a folio, in columns headed 'Iryshe', 'Latten' and 'Englishe'. The first three entries, *aher*, *maher* and *braher* ('father', 'mother' and 'brother'), were discussed in his 'Originall of the nation'; five others *Muri*, *Duine*, *Fear*, *Tala* and *Tenga* ('Mary', 'Person', 'Man', 'Earth' and 'Tongue') do not feature anywhere else in the primer, while *Bean*, *Diá*, *Riuean* ('Woman', 'God', 'Queen') and to some degree *Rí* ('King') appear elsewhere. The inclusion of 'Mary' might seem like a reference to Elizabeth's immediate predecessor and late half-sister, Queen Mary, but Muire (here *Muri*) was used only for the Virgin Mary or similarly named saints, and in compound names; whereas Máire was used for the stand-alone common name.[56] This subtlety would have been lost on Elizabeth and it is difficult to know why Nugent included this item.

The quasi-phonetic orthography of this list seems somewhat out of place, especially in light of Nugent's earlier discussion of mutations in Irish, particularly aspiration, in the 'Originall of the nation'. In the word list he neither uses the superscript lenition symbol nor the letter 'h' to mark lenited consonants, even though he used the former in the letter names in the tabular alphabet.[57] Instead, in the word list he offers phonetic spellings for *athair* 'aher' and *mathair* 'maher', both of which had actually already been used as examples in the 'Originall of the nation'.[58]

The scripts employed in the list are peculiar to each language, with a Gaelic script for Irish, a bookhand for Latin and italic for English (in the case of the latter two, this reverses the usage of the English dedication and Latin 'Originall of the nation'), while the use of different letter forms for *Dia* and *Muri* may be indicative of the religious significance of these names.[59]

Nugent ended the primer with a series of six phrases, which were written in the same quasi-phonetic orthography, language-hand combinations and order as the world list. These appear to be designed for preliminary greeting and then moving onto a common language, and would be suited to the previously suggested scenario of Elizabeth greeting Gaelic Irish nobles. The list is not without its quirks, such as *Abair ladden* for *speake latten*, which might be literally translated as 'say Latin'. That aside, it was undoubtedly intended to begin a conversation in Irish and help it move toward the *lingua franca* of the period, as English (although growing in importance) did not become the dominant language in communication between rebels and the Tudor establishment until the 1580s.[60] The final phrase, *Dia le riuean saxona/God saue the Queene off Englande*, while arguably one Elizabeth might have needed to understand, was certainly included to underline Nugent's loyalty and curry favour with the queen. It is somewhat unusual that he does not call her queen of Ireland, since it was precisely the Anglo-Irish nobility to which Nugent belonged who had pushed for Henry VIII to accept the crown of Ireland.[61]

Notes

Cunningham, *CSPI*	Bernadette Cunningham (ed.), *Calendar of state papers Ireland: Tudor period, 1566–1567* (revised ed., Dublin, 2009).
DIB	James McGuire and James Quinn (eds), *Dictionary of Irish biography from the earliest times to the year 2002* (9 vols, Cambridge, 2009).
Hamilton, *CSPI*	Hans Claude Hamilton (ed.), *Calendar of the state papers relating to Ireland, of the reigns of Henry VIII, Edward VI, Mary, and Elizabeth, 1509–1573* (London, 1860).
History of the University	Victor Morgan (ed.), *A history of the University of Cambridge: volume II, 1546–1750* (Cambridge, 2004).
Lennon, *CSPI*	Colm Lennon (ed.), *Calendar of state papers Ireland: Tudor period, 1547–1553* (revised ed., Dublin, 2015).
ODNB	H.C.G. Matthew and Brian Harrison (eds), *Oxford dictionary of national biography* (60 vols, Oxford, 2004).

A NOTE ON THE TRANSCRIPTIONS

The primer is accessible online at http://www.isos.dias.ie, under 'Marsh's Library'/*Leabharlann an Ardeaspaig Marsh*. All quotations are transcribed from these images, with no alteration or standardization of spelling or punctuation, except that contractions/abbreviations are expanded in italic (or in plain type where English is not the language of the text). References to the primer are simply given in the form 'f. 4v' or 'ff 4v–5r'. All translations from the primer or other sources are my own unless otherwise stated.

INTRODUCTION

1 That speech is available at http://www.dublincastle.ie/History Education/The VisitofHerMajestyQueenElizabethII/FullTextofTheQueensSpeech/#d.en.16153 (accessed 29 Sept. 2015).

2 Benjamin Iveagh Library, IV D1. A digitized version of the manuscript (and catalogue) may be found at http://www.isos.dias.ie (accessed 29 Sept. 2015).

3 For example, despite containing a chapter on Irish in Tudor Ireland, it is not mentioned in Aidan Doyle, *A history of the Irish language: from the Norman invasion to independence* (Oxford, 2015), pp 37–61. The sole exception is Pádraig Ó Macháin, 'Two Nugent manuscripts: the Nugent Duanaire and Queen Elizabeth's Primer', *Ríocht na Midhe*, 23 (2012), 129–38.

4 In terms of linguistic analysis alone, Ó Macháin has noted that 'though slight and ephemeral, his primer, written at the command of Queen Elizabeth, represents, in an inchoate and skeletal form, the beginning of extra-bardic analysis and presentation of the Irish language': Ó Macháin, 'Two Nugent manuscripts', 138.

5 Timothy Corcoran, *Studies in the history of classical teaching: Irish and continental, 1500–1700* (London, 1911), p. 136.

I. THE NUGENTS OF DELVIN

1 Basil Iske [pseudonym of Elizabeth Hickey], *The green cockatrice* (Dublin, 1978), p. 16.

2 Most likely it was sometime later that the feudal barony was deemed to include a peerage, hence the

discrepancy frequently encountered in the numbering of Delvin's lords: Steven G. Ellis, 'Nugent, Richard, third Baron Delvin (*d.* 1538)' in *ODNB.*

3 Colin Veach, *Lordship in four realms: the Lacy Family, 1166–1241* (Manchester, 2014), p. 30.

4 Quoted in G.H. Orpen, *Ireland under the Normans* (4 vols, Oxford, 1911–20), ii, p. 87, and Tomás Ua Brádaigh, 'Telach Cail', *Ríocht na Midhe*, 3:2 (1964), 159–60.

5 Orpen, *Ireland under the Normans*, ii, pp 87–8.

6 For the Nugents' genealogies, see *Leabhar mór na ngenealach (The great book of Irish genealogies) compiled (1645–66) by Dubhaltach Mac Fhirbhisigh*, ed. and trans. Nollaig Ó Muraíle (5 vols, Dublin, 2003), iii, pp 748–59 (§§1401.1–1408.5).

7 Hannah Fitzsimons, *The great Delvin* (2nd ed., Dublin, 1979), p. 21.

8 Orpen, *Ireland under the Normans*, ii, p. 87, n. 5.

9 Peter Crooks (ed.), *A calendar of Irish chancery letters*, c.*1244–1509*, Close Roll 9 Richard II, §17, available at https://chancery.tcd.ie/document/close/9-richard-ii/17 (accessed 29 Sept. 2015).

10 See, for example, ibid., Patent Roll 22 Richard II, §4 (https://chancery.tcd.ie/document/patent/22-richard-ii/4); ibid., Patent Roll 3 Henry IV, §33 (https://chancery.tcd.ie/document/patent/3-henry-iv/33); ibid., Patent Roll 6 Henry IV, §29 (https://chancery.tcd.ie/document/patent/6-henry-iv/29) (accessed 29 Sept. 2015).

11 David Beresford, 'Nugent, Richard' in *DIB*; Elizabeth Matthew, 'Nugent, Richard, first Baron Delvin and baron of Delvin (*d.* 1475)' in *ODNB.* The title of the monarch's proxy in Ireland (earlier known as the justiciar) varies substantially depending on time and the individual holder's prestige; during our period they were mainly titled lord deputy, lord lieutenant or lord justice). For a discussion of the office generally during this period, see Ciaran Brady, 'England's defence and Ireland's reform: the dilemma of the Irish viceroys, 1541–1641' in Brendan Bradshaw and John Morrill (eds), *The British problem, c.1534–1707: state formation in the Atlantic*

archipelago (Basingstoke, 1996), pp 89–117 and Ciaran Brady, 'Viceroys? The Irish chief governors, 1541–1641' in Peter Gray and Olwen Purdue (eds), *The Irish lord lieutenancy, c.1541–1922* (Dublin, 2012), pp 15–42.

12 Crooks, *A calendar of Irish chancery letters*, Patent Roll 16 Edward IV, §3, available at https://chancery.tcd.ie/document/patent/16-edward-iv/3 (accessed 29 Sept. 2015).

13 'H. archbishop of Dublin and Patrick Bermyngham, justice, to Wolsey' in J.S. Brewer (ed.), *Letters and papers, foreign and domestic, of the reign of Henry VIII* (London, 1872), iv (part 2), p. 1757 (§3952).

14 David Beresford, 'Nugent, Richard' in *DIB*; Ellis, 'Nugent, Richard, third Baron Delvin (*d.* 1538)' in *ODNB.*

15 Colm Lennon, 'The Nugent family and the diocese of Kilmore in the sixteenth and early seventeenth centuries', *Breifne*, 9 (1999–2001), 367.

16 'Lord Deputy Croft, Lord Chancellor Cusack and Andrew Wise to the privy council (3 Dec. 1552)' in Lennon, *CSPI*, p. 190 (§397).

17 'Lord Deputy Sussex to the queen (25 Mar. 1558)' in Hamilton, *CSPI*, p. 144 (§31). Confirmation of that grant was duly received: ibid., 'Queen to the lord deputy and chancellor of Ireland (12 Apr. 1558)', p. 144 (§34).

18 Lennon, 'The Nugent family and the diocese of Kilmore', 361–2. For the Nugents involvement with Fore in the 15th and 16th centuries, see Rory Masterson, *Medieval Fore, County Westmeath* (Dublin, 2014), pp 17–18, 48, 50–1, 62–5.

19 Lennon, 'The Nugent family and the diocese of Kilmore', 362. For the case of Fore, see Rory Masterson, 'The alien priory of Fore, Co. Westmeath, in the Middle Ages', *Archivium Hibernicum*, 53 (1999), 73–9.

20 For a brief summary of the abbey under Christopher Nugent's patronage, see Lennon, 'The Nugent family and the diocese of Kilmore', 370–3.

21 Henry Jefferies, *The Irish church and the Tudor Reformations* (Dublin, 2010), pp 257, 271.

22 Terence O'Donnell, *Franciscan abbey of Multyfarnham* (Multyfarnham, 1951), p. 24.

23 Benjamin Hazard, '"An ark in the deluge": Multyfarnham abbey and the Nugents of Delvin, 1607–41', *Ríocht na Midhe*, 22 (2011), 114.

24 Helen Coburn Walshe, 'Responses to the Protestant Reformation in sixteenth-century Meath', *Ríocht na Mídhe*, 8:1 (1987), 106.

25 *Primer* ff 3r–3v. My emphasis.

26 It derives from a Latin neologism coined by Richard Stanihurst in the 1580s (*Anglo-Hibernus*): Jason Harris and Keith Sidwell, 'Introduction: Ireland and *Romanitas*' in Jason Harris and Keith Sidwell (eds), *Making Ireland Roman: Irish neo-Latin writers and the republic of letters* (Cork, 2009), p. 8.

27 See, for, example the stances taken by two of the leading historians of late medieval and Tudor Ireland: Steven G. Ellis, '"More Irish than the Irish themselves"? The "Anglo-Irish" in Tudor Ireland', *History Ireland*, 7:1 (Spring 1999), 22–6 and Kenneth Nicholls, 'Worlds apart? The Ellis two-nation theory on late medieval Ireland', *History Ireland*, 7:2 (Summer 1999), 22–6.

28 Kenneth Nicholls, *Gaelic and Gaelicized Ireland in the Middle Ages* (2nd ed., Dublin, 2003), p. 17.

29 'Duanaire Ghearóid Iarla', ed. Gearóid Mac Niocaill, *Studia Hibernica*, 3 (1963), 7–59.

30 Nicholls, 'Worlds apart?', 25.

31 Ibid., 25–6.

32 Steven G. Ellis, '"More Irish than the Irish themselves"?', 24.

33 Judy Barry, 'Nugent, Christopher (Criostóir Nuinseann)' in *DIB*.

34 Vincent P. Carey, *Surviving the Tudors: the 'wizard' earl of Kildare and English rule in Ireland, 1537–1586* (Dublin, 2002), pp 25–6.

35 Ó Muraíle, *Leabhar mór na ngenealach*, iii, 750–1 (§1402.2).

36 For example, the Powers, Eustaces and Plunkets were all alleged to have descended from Donnchad, son of Brian Boru; see Meidhbhín Ní Úrdail (ed. and trans.), 'A poem on the adventures abroad and death of Donnchadh son of Brian Bóraimhe', *Zeitschrift für celtische Philologie*, 59 (2012), 170–1.

37 Colum Kenny, *King's Inns and the Kingdom of Ireland: the Irish 'Inn of Court', 1541–1800* (Dublin, 1992), p. 34.

38 Lennon, 'The Nugent family and the diocese of Kilmore', 362–7.

39 The word 'colony' is also contested but I believe justified. For an insightful view of the issue, see Brendan Smith, *Colonisation and conquest in medieval Ireland: the English in Louth, 1170–1330* (Cambridge, 1999), pp 1–9.

40 James Hardiman (ed. and trans.), 'A statue of the fortieth year of King Edward III, enacted in a parliament held in Kilkenny, AD 1367, before Lionel duke of Clarence, lord lieutenant of Ireland' in J. Hardiman (ed.), *Tracts relating to Ireland* (2 vols, Dublin, 1841–3), ii, pp 2–121.

41 The issue of bilingualism and its importance for contemporary identities is discussed in Vincent Carey, '"Neither good English nor good Irish": bilingualism and identity formation in sixteenth-century Ireland' in Hiram Morgan (ed.), *Political ideology in Ireland, 1541–1641* (Dublin, 1999), pp 45–61.

42 *Primer* ff 3v–4r.

43 For example, between the 1530s and 1560s three sons of The O'Reilly were married to members of the Nugent family: Lennon, 'The Nugent family and the diocese of Kilmore', 367–8.

44 S.J. Connolly, *Contested island: Ireland, 1460–1630* (Oxford, 2007), p. 37.

45 For details of this poem see Katharine Simms, *Bardic poetry database (Bunachar fhilíocht na scol)* available at http://bardic.celt.dias.ie (§357: *Bronach Goill Bhanbha da eis*) (accessed 29 Sept. 2015). It is translated by Nancy O'Sullivan in Iske, *The green cockatrice*, pp 172–4 (Appendix A: Irish poems and Irish poets). Some brief remarks on it may be found in Ó Macháin, 'Two Nugent manuscripts', 131.

46 Brian Ó Cuív, *The Irish bardic duanaire or 'Poem Book'* (Dublin, 1973), p. 12 (Ó Cuív's translation).

47 The *duanaire* contains poems on a variety of families and Brian Ó Cuív suggested that since all the Nugent poems in it were written by members of the Ó Cobhthaigh family it is possible

that it was originally an Ó Cobhthaigh manuscript and only later came into the possession of the Nugents: ibid., pp 23–4. For William's ownership, see Ó Macháin, 'Two Nugent manuscripts', 125–7.

48 Éamonn Ó Tuathail (ed.), 'Nugentiana', *Éigse*, 2:1 (Spring 1940), 6. For the poem, see Simms, *Bardic poetry database* (§1053: *Geall re hiarlacht ainm baruin*) (accessed 29 Sept. 2015). For a discussion of the poem, see Ó Macháin, 'Two Nugent manuscripts', 130–1.

49 For his Irish-language poetry, see Gerard Murphy (ed. and trans.), 'Poems of exile by Uilliam Nuinseann Mac Barúin Dealbhna', *Éigse*, 6:1 (Winter 1948), 8–15.

50 Marc Caball, 'Faith, culture and sovereignty: Irish nationality and its development, 1558–1625' in Brendan Bradshaw and Peter Roberts (eds), *British consciousness and identity: the making of Britain, 1533–1707* (Cambridge, 1998), p. 119. Despite the industriousness of Elizabeth Hickey and Brian Nugent it seems misguided to think that William Nugent might have been the real William Shakespeare: Iske, *The green cockatrice*; Brian Nugent, *Shakespeare was Irish!* (Meath, 2008).

51 *Holinshed's Irish chronicle: the historie of Irelande from the first inhabitation thereof, vnto the yeare 1509. Collected by Raphaell Holinshed, & continued till the yeare 1547 by Richarde Stanyhurst*, eds Liam Miller and Eileen Power (Dublin, 1979), p. 105.

52 On the identification of Richard see Anne Fogarty, 'Introduction' to Richard Nugent, *Cynthia*, ed. Angelina Lynch (Dublin, 2010), pp 11–19. For a discussion of *Cynthia* that places it in its local and international contexts, see Deirdre Serjeantson, 'Richard Nugent's *Cynthia* (1604): a Catholic sonnet sequence in London, Westmeath and Spanish Flanders' in David Coleman (ed.), *Region, religion and English Renaissance literature* (Aldershot, 2013), pp 67–86.

2. CHRISTOPHER NUGENT, BARON OF DELVIN, 1544–1602

1 On William's and Giolla Brighde's joint education, see Carey, '"Neither good English nor good Irish"', pp 55–6. For

evidence of his continuing closeness to William, see Ó Macháin, 'Two Nugent manuscripts', 127.

2 Lisa Jardine, 'The place of dialectic teaching in sixteenth-century Cambridge', *Studies in the Renaissance*, 21 (1974), 43–4.

3 Diarmaid Ó Catháin, 'Some reflexes of Latin learning and of the Renaissance in Ireland *c.*1450–*c.*1600' in Harris and Sidwell (eds), *Making Ireland Roman*, p. 25.

4 Colm Lennon, 'The print trade, 1550–1700' in Raymond Gillespie and Andrew Hadfield (eds), *The Irish book in English, 1550–1800* (Oxford, 2006), p. 63.

5 Leslie Mahin Oliver, 'A bookseller's account book, 1545', *Harvard Library Bulletin*, 16:2 (April 1968), 143–51.

6 Fergal McGrath, *Education in ancient and medieval Ireland* (Dublin, 1979), pp 195–6.

7 For the English dialects of Ireland, see Alan Bliss, 'The English language in early modern Ireland' in T.W. Moody, F.X. Martin and F.J. Byrne (eds), *A new history of Ireland, iii: early modern Ireland, 1534–1691* (Oxford, 1976), pp 546–60.

8 His death was noted late in the year: 'Memorandum on the decease of Richard Baron Delvin (8 Dec. 1559)' in Hamilton, *CSPI*, p. 157 (§76).

9 Ibid., 'Lord Lieutenant Sussex to Cecil (13 Mar. 1563)', p. 213 (§17).

10 Elizabeth Hickey speculated that Christopher's own father may have been a ward of Thomas Cromwell, but the grounds for this suggestion are unspecified: Iske, *The green cockatrice*, p. 16.

11 Charles Henry Cooper and Thompson Cooper, *Athenae Cantabrigienses* (2 vols, Cambridge, 1858–61), ii, pp 331–3. There had been some family tradition of education in England, as Christopher's uncle, Nicholas, had entered Lincoln's Inn in 1558: Colm Lennon, 'Nugent, Nicholas (d. 1582)' in *ODNB*. Indeed, by the 1550s the number of students from Ireland in the universities had increased substantially, particularly in the law: Connolly, *Contested island*, p. 129.

12 On this policy and Sussex's viceroyalty generally, see Ciaran Brady, *The chief governors: the rise and fall of reform government in Tudor Ireland, 1536–1588* (Cambridge, 1994), pp 72–112. Clare Hall

is now known as Clare College and is not to be confused with the modern Clare Hall (founded in 1966).

13 Primer f. 3r.

14 Seán P. Ó Mathúna, *William Bathe, S.J., 1564–1614: a pioneer in linguistics* (Amsterdam and Philadelphia, 1986), pp 147–8.

15 Quoted in John Patrick Montaño, *The roots of English colonialism in Ireland* (Cambridge, 2011), p. 353, n. 43. Indeed, negotiations in Whitehall were conducted through a series of translated position papers: Patricia Palmer, 'Interpreters and the politics of translation and traduction in sixteenth-century Ireland', *Irish Historical Studies*, 33:1 (May 2003), 271.

16 Ó Mathúna, *William Bathe*, pp 147–8.

17 Victor Morgan, 'Cambridge University and the State' in *History of the University*, pp 108–9.

18 Victor Morgan and Christopher Brooke, 'Prologue: Cambridge saved' in *History of the University*, p. 11. Indeed seven members of Elizabeth's privy council (and many more lower-rank administrators) had studied at Cambridge: Felicity Heal, *Reformation in Britain and Ireland* (Oxford, 2003), p. 232.

19 Victor Morgan, 'The constitutional revolution of the 1570s' in *History of the University*, p. 65.

20 Wallace T. MacCaffrey, 'Radcliffe, Thomas, third earl of Sussex (1526/7–1583)' in *ODNB*.

21 'Hugh Brady, bishop of Meath, to Sir William Cecil (27 Oct. 1567)' in Cunningham, *CSPI*, p. 225 (§546).

22 Ibid., 'Lords Justice Weston and Fitzwilliam and council to the privy council (27 Oct. 1567)', pp 225–6 (§547).

23 It is unfortunate that the name of Nugent's tutor is unknown, as tutors and students often had close relationships, sharing rooms and presumably books too: Elisabeth S. Leedham-Green (ed.), *Books in Cambridge inventories: book-lists from vice-chancellor's court probate inventories in the Tudor and Stuart periods* (2 vols, Cambridge, 1986), i, pp xxiii–xxiv. See also, Victor Morgan and Christopher Brooke, 'Tutors and students' in *History of the University*, pp 314–42.

24 Morgan, 'Cambridge University and the state', pp 131–2.

25 Ibid., pp 117–18.

26 Ibid., pp 133–4.

27 In addition, it should be noted that it was only in the 1570s that an explicit linking of Catholicism and Gaelic culture began to gain momentum: Caball, 'Faith, culture and sovereignty', p. 132. Furthermore, the earliest printed Protestant texts in Gaelic (from the late 1560s to the first decade of the following century) demonstrate that 'there was no inherent cleavage in this phase of the reformation between Gaelic culture and Protestantism': Marc Caball, 'Gaelic and Protestant: a case study in early modern self-fashioning, 1567–1608', *Proceedings of the Royal Irish Academy*, 110C (2010), 214.

28 Richard Rex, *Elizabeth I: fortune's bastard: a short account of the long life of Elizabeth I* (Stroud, 2003), pp 54–60; Walshe, 'Responses to the Protestant Reformation', 100.

29 Morgan, 'The constitutional revolution of the 1570s', pp 64–7. See also, H.C. Porter, *Reformation and reaction in Tudor Cambridge* (Cambridge, 1958), pp 101–7.

30 Victor Morgan, 'The electoral scene and the court: royal mandates, 1558–1640' in *History of the University*, p. 389.

31 John T. Gilbert (ed.), *Facsimiles of national manuscripts of Ireland* (5 vols, London, 1874–84), iv (part 1), pp xxxv–xxxviii.

32 Ibid., p. xxxv (§7). I have been unable to trace the precise source of Nugent's version of the Vulgate's Luke 11:17.

33 *John Nichols's The progresses and public processions of Queen Elizabeth I: a new edition of the early modern sources. Volume 1: 1533–1571*, eds Elizabeth Goldring, Faith Eales, Elizabeth Clarke and Jayne Elisabeth Archer (5 vols, Oxford, 2014), i, pp 375–437.

34 Zillah Dovey, *An Elizabethan progress: the queen's journey into East Anglia, 1578* (Stroud, 1996), p. 1.

35 Jean Wilson, *Entertainments for Elizabeth I* (Woodbridge, 1980), p. 143, n. 19.

36 Marion Colthorpe, *Royal Cambridge: royal visitors to Cambridge: Queen Elizabeth I – Queen Elizabeth II* (Cambridge, 1977), p. 1.

37 Morgan, 'Cambridge University and the state', p. 119.

38 The university was given very little notice of the visitation; it was only informed in mid-July: Jane Osborne, *Entertaining Elizabeth I: the progresses and great houses of her time* (London, 1989), p. 54.

39 *John Nichols' The progresses and public processions of Queen Elizabeth I*, eds Goldring et al., i, p. 434. Both Sussex and Hunsdon were made MAs before leaving, as were various other aristocratic members of Elizabeth's entourage: ibid., 433. Christopher's younger brother, William, attended Hart Hall in Oxford, which may also suggest that Sussex was not unduly close to Cambridge.

40 Ibid., 416. For Welles' oration, see: ibid., 416, n. 181.

41 Ibid., 401–7. *Pace* Morgan, there seems no reason to believe that the primer was produced in 1562 or that Nugent was at the Inns of Court at the time: Hiram Morgan, '"Never any realm worse governed": Queen Elizabeth and Ireland', *Transactions of the Royal Historical Society*, 14 (2004), 296. Palmer too opts for a 1562 date (on unstated grounds): see 'Interpreters and the politics of translation', 277 and Patricia Palmer, *Language and conquest in early modern Ireland: English Renaissance literature and Elizabethan imperial expansion* (Cambridge, 2001), p. 81.

42 Elisabeth Leedham-Green, *Verses presented to Queen Elizabeth I by the University of Cambridge, August 1564, Cambridge University Library MS Add. 8915* (Cambridge, 1993), pp i–ii.

43 Ibid., pp ii–iii.

44 The Clare Hall contributions are found on ff 147r–60v and are catalogued in ibid., pp 32–5.

45 *John Nichols's The progresses and public processions of Queen Elizabeth I*, eds Goldring et al., i, p. 437. Ó Cearnaigh did not provide verses for the surviving volume commissioned by Cecil, as members of Magdalen College and Trinity Hall abstained from doing so: Leedham-Green, *Verses presented to Queen Elizabeth I*, pp ii–iii.

46 Patrick Collinson, *Elizabeth I* (Oxford, 2007), pp 7–8; Patrick Collinson, 'Elizabeth I (1533–1603)' in *ODNB*.

47 Collinson, 'Elizabeth I (1533–1603)' in *ODNB*.

48 There is no way of knowing for certain if Nugent knew of Elizabeth's own codicological efforts; his binding of the primer in vellum might suggest that he did not (Elizabeth preferred velvet over leather or vellum): Leedham-Green, *Verses presented to Queen Elizabeth I*, p. i, n. 3.

49 David Loades, 'Foreword' to Dovey, *An Elizabethan progress*, p. x.

50 Anne Somerset, *Elizabeth I* (London, 1997), p. 10.

51 Ibid., p. 11.

52 Collinson, *Elizabeth I*, p. 7.

53 Somerset, *Elizabeth I*, pp 11–12.

54 Ibid., pp 10–11.

55 Leedham-Green, *Verses presented to Queen Elizabeth I*, p. ii.

56 Primer ff 2r–4v.

57 His landholdings had increased during his time at Cambridge and Judy Barry has rightly characterized the favour shown to him by the government as a policy of 'careful grooming': Judy Barry, 'Nugent, Christopher (Criostóir Nuinseann) in *DIB*. See, for example, *The Irish fiants of the Tudor sovereigns during the reigns of Henry VIII, Edward VI, Philip & Mary, and Elizabeth I* (4 vols, Dublin, 1994), ii, p. 55 (§486).

58 In addition to not needing a degree in the manner that less prosperous students might, Nugent may have balked at the idea of swearing the mandatory oath denying papal authority required of everyone proceeding to a degree (as required since 1536): Morgan, 'Cambridge University and the state', p. 107, n. 34.

59 In November the queen granted these and sent instructions to Lord Deputy Sidney regarding his return: 'Queen to Lord Deputy Sidney (22 Nov. 1565)' in Hamilton, *CSPI*, p. 279 (§47). The abbey had already been in the Nugents' hands since the dissolution: Walshe, 'Responses to the Protestant Reformation', 106.

60 *The Irish fiants*, ii, p. 91 (§838).

61 Two years later he claimed that his estate was encumbered by a jointure to his mother and his father's debts: 'Sir Christopher Nugent, Baron Delvin

to privy council (23 Mar. 1567)' in Cunningham, *CSPI*, p. 167 (§387).

62 Ibid., 'Thomas Lancaster to Sir William Cecil (23 Nov. 1566)', p. 136 (§298).

63 Ibid., 'Lord Deputy Sidney to privy council (10 Jan. 1567)', p. 151 (§336).

64 Ibid., 'Sir Christopher Nugent, Baron Delvin to privy council (23 Mar. 1567)', p. 167 (§387).

65 Ibid., 'Queen Elizabeth to Lord Deputy Sidney (10 May 1567)', p. 182 (§432). See also ibid., 'Note of Baron Delvin's supplication (10 May 1567)', p. 182 (§433).

66 Lennon, 'The Nugent family and the diocese of Kilmore', 368–9.

67 Walshe, 'Responses to the Protestant Reformation', 106.

68 Iske, *The green cockatrice*, pp 23–4.

69 For Derrick's images, see http://www. docs.is.ed.ac.uk/docs/lib-archive/ bgallery/Gallery/researchcoll/ireland. html (accessed 29 Sept. 2015).

70 Colm Lennon, 'Nugent, Christopher, fifth Baron Delvin (1544–1602)' in *ODNB*.

71 Jon G. Crawford, *Anglicizing the government of Ireland: the Irish privy council and the expansion of Tudor rule, 1556–1578* (Dublin, 1993), p. 123.

72 For a discussion of the cess and the role it played in the larger relationships between the Palesmen and the administration, see Ciaran Brady, 'Conservative subversives: the community of the Pale and the Dublin administration, 1556–86' in Patrick J. Corish (ed.), *Radicals, rebels & establishments, Historical Studies XV* (Belfast, 1985), pp 11–32.

73 Helen Coburn Walshe, 'The rebellion of William Nugent, 1581' in R.V. Comerford, Mary Cullen, Jacqueline R. Hill and Colm Lennon (eds), *Religion, conflict and coexistence in Ireland: essays presented to Monsignor Patrick J. Corish* (Dublin, 1990), pp 26–52. For Nugent's own tacit involvement, see Jefferies, *The Irish church and the Tudor Reformations*, pp 214–19.

74 Walshe, 'The rebellion of William Nugent, 1581', 52.

75 Joseph Foster (ed.), *The register of admissions to Gray's Inn, 1521–1889, together with the register of marriages in Gray's Inn chapel, 1695–1754* (London, 1889), p. 66.

76 For the murder of Nugent's uncle, Nicholas, see Lennon, 'Nugent, Nicholas (d. 1582)' in *ODNB* and Judy Barry, 'Nugent, Nicholas', in *DIB*. Dillon also received Nicholas Nugent's lands after the latter's execution, which doubtless made him even more execrable in Christopher's eyes: Walshe, 'Responses to the Protestant Reformation', 103.

77 Lennon, 'The Nugent family and the diocese of Kilmore', 372. For the campaign against Dillon, see Jon G. Crawford, *A Star Chamber court in Ireland: the court of Castle Chamber, 1571–1641* (Dublin, 2005), pp 268–9.

78 Jefferies, *The Irish church and the Tudor Reformations*, pp 237–9, 271–5; Palmer, 'Interpreters and the politics of translation', 266, 272–3.

79 Judy Barry, 'Nugent, Christopher (Criostóir Nuinseann)' in *DIB*.

80 For his will and post mortem inquisition, see John F. Ainsworth and Edward MacLysaght (eds), 'Survey of documents in private keeping, second series', *Analecta Hibernica*, 29 (1958), 133–5.

81 Hazard, '"An ark in the deluge"', 113–23.

82 Lennon, 'Nugent, Christopher, fifth Baron Delvin (1544–1602)' in *ODNB*.

3. ATTITUDES TO IRISH IN THE 16TH CENTURY

1 Palmer, 'Interpreters and the politics of translation', 258.

2 Palmer, *Language and conquest in early modern Ireland*, p. 8.

3 Ibid., pp 80–1.

4 'Ordinances proclaimed by Lord Deputy Sidney for the benefit of the Irish countries, and committed to the seneschals to be observed through all Leinster, Meath, and Westmeath (15 Apr. 1566)' in Cunningham, *CSPI*, pp 43–4 (§84.1).

5 Ibid., 'Memorandum of agreement between the earl of Thomond and Donal O'Brien (1567)', pp 170–1 (§397).

6 For an overview of the study of 'Surrender and Regrant', see Christopher Maginn, '"Surrender and Regrant" in the historiography of sixteenth-century Ireland', *The Sixteenth-Century Journal*, 38:4 (2007), 955–74.

7 William Camden, *Annales: the true and royall history of the famous Empresse Elizabeth*, trans. Abraham Darcie (London, 1625), p. 90.

8 Ciaran Brady, *Shane O'Neill* (Dundalk, 1996), p. 38. Shane's visit is discussed at pp 37–41.

9 James Hogan, 'Shane O'Neill comes to the Court of Elizabeth' in Séamus Pender (ed.), *Féilscríbhinn Torna .i. Tráchtaisí léanta in onóir don Ollamh Tadhg Ua Donnchadha, D.Litt. (Essays and studies presented to Professor Tadhg Ua Donnchadha (Torna))* (Cork, 1947), p. 166, n. 58.

10 Ibid., p. 168.

11 McGrath, *Education in ancient and medieval Ireland*, pp 152–3.

12 Primer f. 10v. Judging by travellers' accounts from around 1600, the Irish emerge as some of the most proficient Latin speakers in Europe: Ó Catháin, 'Some reflexes of Latin learning', p. 18.

13 This was by no means solely a Protestant concern; one outcome of the Council of Trent (1545–63) was that preaching in the vernacular also became a central aspect of the Counter-Reformation: Palmer, *Language and conquest in early modern Ireland*, pp 36–7.

14 Felicity Heal, 'Mediating the word: language and dialects in the British and Irish Reformations', *Journal of Ecclesiastical History*, 56:2 (2005), 267–8.

15 Ibid., 264.

16 Nonetheless, in 1575 the president of Magdalen College, Oxford, supposedly presented Elizabeth with a copy of the scriptures in Irish, which allegedly had been translated by the 14th century archbishop of Armagh, Richard FitzRalph: ibid., 277–8.

17 *Aibidil Gaoidheilge & Caiticiosma: Seaán Ó Cearnaigh's Irish primer of religion, published in 1571*, ed. Brian Ó Cuív (Dublin, 1994).

18 Quoted in Heal, 'Mediating the word', 276. It might be compared to Spanish attitudes to Native American tongues, which they sought to control rather than empower: Palmer, *Language and conquest in early modern Ireland*, pp 37–8.

19 Morgan, '"Never any realm worse governed"', 296. It is not entirely clear

who the intended recipients of this gesture were.

20 Ciaran Brady, 'Court, castle and country: the framework of government in Tudor Ireland' in Ciaran Brady and Raymond Gillespie (eds), *Natives and newcomers: essays on the making of Irish colonial society, 1534–1641* (Dublin, 1986), p. 23. The very use of the word 'policy' is somewhat problematic, as it carries with it modern connotations of clearly defined, authoritative official attitudes.

21 Thomas O'Connor, 'Religious change, 1550–1800' in Raymond Gillespie and Andrew Hadfield (eds), *The Irish book in English, 1550–1800* (Oxford, 2006), p. 173.

22 Marc Caball, 'Print, Protestantism, and cultural authority in Elizabethan Ireland' in Brendan Kane and Valerie McGowan-Doyle (eds), *Elizabeth I and Ireland* (Cambridge, 2014), p. 291.

23 Heal, *Reformation in Britain and Ireland*, p. 381.

24 Quoted in Heal, 'Mediating the word', 279.

25 Heal, *Reformation in Britain and Ireland*, p. 384.

26 Caball, 'Gaelic and Protestant', 195.

27 T.C. Barnard, 'Protestants and the Irish language, c.1675–1725', *Journal of Ecclesiastical History*, 44:2 (1993), 247.

4. CONTEXTS OF THE PRIMER

1 In the 1540s an Englishman named Andrew Borde published a book of national character sketches, which included a short section on Ireland and a bilingual number and phrase list (in English and Irish) which appears to have been intended to enable a traveller (and very likely soldier) to order food in his lodgings and pay the bill, but this did not have any pedagogical element: Andrew Borde, *The fyrst boke of the introduction of knowledge*, ed. James Hogg (2 vols, Salzburg, 1979), ii, pp 21–4.

2 George Calder (ed. and trans.), *Auraicept na n-éces: The scholars' primer* (Edinburgh, 1917); Anders Ahlqvist (ed. and trans.), *The early Irish linguist: an edition of the canonical part of the Auraicept na néces* (Helsinki, 1983). For a brief summary of the history of the study of language

in Ireland up to the end of the 17th century, see Ahlqvist, *The early Irish linguist*, pp 7–21.

3 Ahlqvist, *The early Irish linguist*, p. 17.

4 Osborn Bergin (ed.), 'Irish grammatical tracts', published as supplements to *Ériu*, 8, 9, 10, 14 and 17 (1916–55); Eoin Mac Cárthaigh (ed. and trans.), *The art of bardic poetry: a new edition of Irish grammatical tracts I* (Dublin, 2014); Lambert McKenna (ed.), *Bardic syntactical tracts* (Dublin, 1944).

5 Damian McManus, 'An Nua-Ghaeilge Chlasaiceach' in Kim McCone, Damian McManus, Cathal Ó Háinle, Nicholas Williams and Liam Breatnach (eds), *Stair na Gaeilge in ómós do Pádraig Ó Fiannachta* (Maynooth, 1994), p. 335 (§1.1).

6 Bergin, 'Irish grammatical tracts', Supplement to *Ériu*, 8 (1916), ii.

7 On Elizabethan attitudes to the poets, see Marc Caball, 'Innovation and tradition: Irish Gaelic responses to early modern conquest and colonization' in Hiram Morgan (ed.), *Political ideology in Ireland, 1541–1641* (Dublin, 1999), pp 62–70.

8 Bergin, 'Irish grammatical tracts', supplement to *Ériu*, 8 (1916), ii.

9 Ó Mathúna, *William Bathe*, p. 78.

10 For Ó Mathúna's suggested links between the two, see ibid., pp xi–xii, 80, 147–9. See also Seán P. Ó Mathúna, 'Bathe, William' in *DIB*. He was followed by Palmer, *Language and conquest in early modern Ireland*, p. 8.

11 Ó Mathúna, *William Bathe*, p. 147.

12 Nicholas Orme, 'Schools and schoolmasters (to *c.*1550)' in Elisabeth Leedham-Green and Teresa Webber (eds), *The Cambridge history of libraries in Britain and Ireland, volume I, to 1640* (Cambridge, 2006), pp 431–2.

13 Primer f. 3r.

14 Primer ff 3v–4r. The parenthesis does not close.

15 Mary Ann Lyons, *Gearóid Óg, ninth earl of Kildare* (Dublin, 1998), p. 20.

16 For Bathe's detailed discussion of how he conceived his work, see the preface to *Ianua Linguarum*: Sean F. O'Mahony [Seán P. Ó Mathúna], 'The preface to William Bathe's *Ianua Linguarum* (1611)', *Historiographia Linguistica*, 8:1 (1981), 131–64.

17 Ó Mathúna, *William Bathe*, p. 123.

18 W. Keith Percival, 'Changes in the approach to language' in Norman Kretzmann, Anthony Kenny and Jan Pinborg (eds), *The Cambridge history of later medieval philosophy: from the rediscovery of Aristotle to the disintegration of scholasticism, 1100–1600* (Cambridge, 1982), pp 812–13.

19 Ó Mathúna, *William Bathe*, pp 130–5.

20 Gabriel Nuchelmans, 'Logic in the seventeenth century: preliminary remarks and the constituents of the proposition' in Daniel Garber and Michael Ayers (eds), *The Cambridge history of seventeenth-century philosophy* (2 vols, Cambridge, 1998), i, p. 104.

21 For Ramus and the diagrammatic structure, see Bradin Cormack and Carla Mazzio, *Book use, book theory: 1500–1700* (Chicago, 2005), pp 67–9.

22 Elisabeth Leedham-Green, *A concise history of the University of Cambridge* (Cambridge, 1996), p. 38.

23 Ibid., pp 38–9.

24 Ibid., pp 37–9.

25 Christopher Brooke, 'Learning and doctrine, 1550–1660' in *History of the University*, p. 437.

26 For a discussion of the tutor-student relationship, see Morgan and Brooke, 'Tutors and students', pp 314–42.

27 MacCaffrey, 'Radcliffe, Thomas, third earl of Sussex (1526/7–1583)' in *ODNB*.

28 Jardine, 'The place of dialectic teaching', 32–3, 50.

29 Ibid., 43.

30 Ibid., 57.

31 Ibid., 51.

32 Ó Macháin, 'Two Nugent manuscripts', 133. On Donatus (and commentators upon him) see Vivien Law, *The history of linguistics in Europe from Plato to 1600* (Cambridge, 2003), pp 65–83.

33 David McKitterick, 'Libraries and the organisation of knowledge' in Leedham-Green and Webber (eds), *The Cambridge history of libraries*, i, pp 592–3.

34 Roger Lovatt, 'College and university book collections and libraries', in Leedham-Green and Webber (eds), *The Cambridge history of libraries*, i, p. 168.

35 Leedham-Green, *Books in Cambridge inventories*, i, p. xx.

36 Ibid., i, 311–13 (§134).

37 Although a new arrival, Welles' position second in the list of Clare Hall contributors to the volume presented to Elizabeth (ahead of Nugent in fourth) suggests he was considered one of the most important members of the college. For a list of the contributors, see Leedham-Green, *Verses presented to Queen Elizabeth I*, pp 32–5.

38 Jardine, 'The place of dialectic teaching', 34.

39 Leedham-Green, *Books in Cambridge inventories*, i, p. 311 (§134).

40 Cooper and Cooper, *Athenae Cantabrigienses*, ii, 304–5 and 552 (Ó Cearnaigh (as John Kearney)) and 331–3 (Nugent).

41 Nicholas Williams, *I bprionta i leabhar: na Protastúin agus prós na Gaeilge, 1567–1724* (Dublin, 1986), p. 24.

42 Ó Macháin, 'Two Nugent manuscripts', 138.

43 For the diphthongs see Primer f. 9r and Ó Cuív, *Aibidil*, pp 64–7 [9–10].

44 In contrast, it is not found in the alphabet supplied by the former poet Giolla Brighde Ó hEódhasa in his *Rudimenta grammaticae Hibernicae*: Parthalán Mac Aogáin (ed.), *Graiméir Ghaeilge na mBráthar Mionúr*, (Dublin, 1968), p. 4.

45 Ó Macháin, 'Two Nugent manuscripts', 134.

46 Morgan, 'Cambridge University and the state', pp 138–46.

47 Morgan and Brooke, 'Tutors and students', pp 329–30.

48 Peter Cunich, David Hoyle, Eamon Duffy and Ronald Hyam, *A history of Magdalene College Cambridge, 1428–1988* (Cambridge, 1994), pp 47–9.

49 Leedham-Green, *A concise history of the University of Cambridge*, pp 62, 243.

50 Ibid., pp 62–3, 245–6.

5. CONTENTS OF THE PRIMER

1 Leedham-Green, *Verses presented to Queen Elizabeth I*, p. iv.

2 The verse volume is now Cambridge University Library, MS Add. 8915. The thread is largely missing but the knots on the inside covers are still present underneath a pasted-down sheet and the colour may be discerned from where they were clipped on the outside of the covers.

3 Leedham-Green, *Verses presented to Queen Elizabeth I*, p. iv.

4 Ibid., p. iv. That the binding is contemporary is suggested by the presence of the same oval design on a 1563 two-volume copy of Aristotle's works found in St John's College, Cambridge, MS Cc.8. 11–12.

5 Ann Moss, *Printed commonplace-books and the structuring of Renaissance thought* (Oxford, 1996), p. 103.

6 Cormack and Mazzio, *Book use, book theory*, p. 49.

7 Richard A. McCabe, 'Ireland's Eliza: queen or *caillech*?' in Brendan Kane and Valerie McGowan-Doyle (eds), *Elizabeth I and Ireland* (Cambridge, 2014), p. 23.

8 Ibid., p. 24.

9 Cormack and Mazzio, *Book use, book theory*, p. 79.

10 Palmer, 'Interpreters and the politics of translation', 257.

11 Cormack and Mazzio, *Book use, book theory*, p. 62.

12 Elizabeth Zouche's grandmother was Margaret's half-sister: Michael K. Jones and Malcolm G. Underwood, *The king's mother: Lady Margaret Beaufort, countess of Richmond and Derby* (Cambridge, 1992), p. 84.

13 Aisling Byrne, 'The earls of Kildare and their books at the end of the Middle Ages', *The Library*, 14:2 (2013), 140.

14 Brendan Kane and Valerie McGowan-Doyle, 'Elizabeth I and Ireland: an introduction' in Kane and McGowan-Doyle (eds), *Elizabeth I and Ireland*, p. 1.

15 Caball, 'Print, Protestantism, and cultural authority', p. 305.

16 Ibid., p. 304.

17 Ó Macháin, 'Two Nugent manuscripts', 135. Even so, their very presence indicates the influence of print culture.

18 Ibid., 138.

19 Primer f. 3r.

20 Ó Macháin, 'Two Nugent manuscripts', 133.

21 R.A.S. Macalister (ed. and trans.), *Lebor gabála Érenn: The book of the taking of Ireland* (5 vols, Dublin 1938–56); Gerald

of Wales, *The history and topography of Ireland*, trans. John J. O'Meara (revised ed., London, 1982), pp 98–9 (§91).

22 Harris and Sidwell, 'Introduction: Ireland and *Romanitas*', p. 4.

23 His numbering does not quite square with that of the published translation of the first recension and further investigation may indicate the recension Nugent used.

24 *Pace* Ó Macháin, 'Two Nugent manuscripts', 134. On reading Gerald, see Aisling Byrne, 'Family, locality, and nationality: vernacular adaptations of the *Expugnatio Hibernica* in late medieval Ireland', *Medium Aevum*, 82:1 (2013), 101–18; Hiram Morgan, 'Giraldus Cambrensis and the Tudor conquest of Ireland' in Hiram Morgan (ed.), *Political ideology in Ireland, 1541–1641* (Dublin, 1999), pp 22–44. I am grateful to Dr Byrne for supplying me with an offprint of her article.

25 For the writing of history in that period, see Alan Ford, '"Standing one's ground": religion, polemic and Irish history since the Reformation' in Alan Ford, James McGuire and Kenneth Milne (eds), *As by law established: the Church of Ireland since the Reformation* (Dublin, 1995), pp 1–14, and Alan Ford, 'The Irish historical renaissance and the shaping of Protestant history' in Alan Ford and John McCafferty (eds), *The origins of sectarianism in early modern Ireland* (Cambridge, 2005), pp 127–57.

26 For details, see Ó Macháin, 'Two Nugent manuscripts', 133–4.

27 The dropping of a letter or syllable at the start of a word.

28 Primer f. 6v.

29 Leedham-Green, *A concise history of the University of Cambridge*, pp 48–9.

30 Victor Morgan, 'Cambridge and "The Country"', in *History of the university*, p. 213.

31 Quoted in Heal, 'Mediating the word', 272.

32 Quoted in ibid.

33 Barnard, 'Protestants and the Irish language', 245–6. See also, Umberto Eco (trans. James Fentress), *The search for the perfect language* (London, 1995).

34 The use of gothic text for 'the Irish alphabet' ending in a fleuron/hedera (a leaf like device for punctuation and ornamental purposes common in printing) and Roman and Italic for everything else, indicates an indebtedness to English primers, as does the inclusion of the alphabet itself in upper and lower case: Ó Macháin, 'Two Nugent manuscripts', 135.

35 Ibid., 135.

36 Ó Cuív, *Aibidil*, pp 58–9 [6].

37 Ian Green, '"The necessary knowledge of the principles of religion": catechisms and catechizing in Ireland, *c*.1560–1800' in Ford, McGuire and Milne (eds), *As by law established*, p. 72.

38 Orme, 'Schools and schoolmasters (to *c*.1550)', p. 420.

39 Caball, 'Print, Protestantism, and cultural authority', p. 290.

40 On 'q' and its relationship to *ceart*, see Damian McManus, *A guide to Ogam* (Maynooth, 1991), pp 33–4 (§3.13) and 37 (§3.15).

41 Ó Cuív, *Aibidil*, pp 58–61 [6–7].

42 McManus, *A guide to Ogam*, p. 34 (§3.14).

43 Ibid., p. 35 (§3.14b–e).

44 On tall 'e' denoting 'ea', see Bergin, 'Irish grammatical tracts', supplement to *Ériu*, 8 (1916), iii and Mac Cárthaigh, *The art of bardic poetry*, p. 23, n. 38.

45 Mac Aogáin, *Graiméir Ghaeilge na mBráthar Mionúr*, p. 3. On *peithe/peithbog*, see McManus, *A guide to Ogam*, p. 184, n. 49.

46 Ó Macháin, 'Two Nugent manuscripts', 136.

47 Uppercase 'K' and 'R' appear to pose something of a palaeographic problem. The Gaelic 'K' and 'R' of the table do not correspond with those of the linear alphabet. The 'R' of the tabular alphabet is clearly not the 'r' of the linear alphabet, but rather quite similar to the 'k' of the linear alphabet and elsewhere Nugent tends to vary his use of the two forms of 'r'. The only other example of 'k' in the primer appears to be a mix of the two 'k's (found on f. 8v).

48 Ó Cuív, *Aibidil*, pp 62–3 [8]; Ó Cuív's translation, p. 161.

49 Ibid., p. 14.

50 Ó Macháin, 'Two Nugent manuscripts', 137.

51 Ibid., 136.
52 On the vowels and consonants in Classical Modern Irish, see McManus, 'An Nua-Ghaeilge Chlasaiceach', pp 344–50 (§§2.2–2.9) and 351–60 (§§2.10–3.5).
53 Ó Macháin, 'Two Nugent manuscripts', 136.
54 Ó Cuív, *Aibidil*, pp 161–3.
55 Mac Aogáin, *Graiméir Ghaeilge na mBráthar Mionúr*, p. 4.
56 Brian Ó Cuív, 'Aspects of Irish personal names', *Celtica*, 18 (1986), 165.
57 Primer f. 8r. Lenited consonants are marked in the names for the letters 'b', 'e', 'h', 'i' and 'p'.
58 Spelled *mathir* in the 'Originall of the nation'. Note also the change of 'ai' to 'e'.
59 I am grateful to Prof. Eamonn Duffy (University of Cambridge) for the latter suggestion.
60 Palmer, 'Interpreters and the politics of translation', 260.
61 I am grateful to Prof. Raymond Gillespie (Maynooth University) for this observation.